T0207567

REVOLUTION IN THE REVOLUTION?

ARMED STRUGGLE AND POLITICAL STRUGGLE IN LATIN AMERICA

RÉGIS DEBRAY

Translated from the author's French
and Spanish by Bobbye Ortiz

VERSO

This English-language edition published by Verso 2017
First English-language edition published 1967
Originally published in French as *Révolution dans la révolution?* 1967
© Régis Debray 1967, 2017
Translation of the preface to the Verso edition © Gregory Elliott 2017

1 3 5 7 9 10 8 6 4 2

Verso
UK: 6 Meard Street, London W1F 0EG
USA: 388 Atlantic Ave, Brooklyn, NY 11217
www.versobooks.com

Verso is the imprint of New Left Books

ISBN-13: 978-1-78663-403-0
ISBN-13: 978-1-78663-404-7 (UK EBK)
ISBN-13: 978-1-78663-405-4 (US EBK)

British Library Cataloguing in Publication Data
A catalogue record for this book is available from the British Library

Library of Congress Cataloging-in-Publication Data
A catalog record for this book is available from the Library of Congress

Printed in the United States

CONTENTS

PREFACE TO THE VERSO EDITION

Works of literature can, and must, transcend the circumstances of their publication. Political writings do not have this faculty: they have an expiry date. They are wagers on the future, laid instinctively, in the excitement of a unique, unrepeatable moment, when form is not available to sublimate content, for they are generally bereft of style or captive to a logomachy peculiar to their time. Composed in a 'Marxist-Leninist' idiom, *Revolution in the Revolution?* all too evidently falls into this category.

The collective wager of which this pamphlet was intended to be a mere prop was not won. I myself registered this some years later, in *A Critique of Arms* (1974), a self-critical work. Fifty years after 1967, 'the hour of the furnaces' appears to us to have been extinguished in a bloodbath. The political and social rights won by the Latin American nations, the end of the dictatorships, the restoration of freedom – these were not achieved by armed vanguards, but by the reconstruction of trades unions, implantation in the shanty towns, and the revival of united opposition fronts and specifically political organizations. When *Revolution in the Revolution?* was conceived and distributed, the democratic process was completely blocked and state repression presaged the worst, as indicated by the murder of the wounded Che and, in a longer time frame, the 1970s, with Pinochet's coup d'état in Chile, the Argentine and Brazilian dictatorships, the Condor Plan, and the liquidation without trial of opponents. Today, it is obvious that armed struggle and the theory of the *foco* were not correct responses to this situation. But it is also a fact that the gesture of insurrection and the example of the *guerillero heroico* served as a moral and symbolic spur to the more or less popular uprisings that put an end to the oligarchical terror in subsequent decades. The great figures of history are more powerful dead than alive, as attested in their different ways by a Guevara or a de Gaulle.

The small, portable textbook that Verso has decided to reprint thus belongs to history. Its value is that of a document, testimony to an era when the whiff of gunpowder was ubiquitous – Algeria, Vietnam, Cuba, Mozambique, Angola – and which Europeans under the age of sixty cannot but find hard to imagine. The climate of a historical moment suffers from the same defect as jazz tunes, love affairs and rages: they are difficult to share, or even understand, retrospectively, except through novels or films. That is why it is cruel to ask the author of a faded love letter to a pretty young woman who has since become an unattractive old lady to preface it half a century later.

The lady in question is the idea of Revolution. It represented a summons to the present from the future – a future as imperious as it was imprecise, swimming in a haze amenable to every kind of imaginary projection, whose supporters were careful not to examine the content or outcome, but of which they could have taken the measure in the so-called socialist countries. Such is the magic of the word, which today is conjugated solely in the imperfect, but which yesterday was only employed in the future by those who believed in it. Despite its recent invention – two centuries at most – we must recognize in this myth of convocation the turbid ambivalence of the *sovereign God* among followers of revealed religions: the same charge of energy, the same dynamic power, bearer at once of a surplus of life and a surplus of death; a surplus of generosity and abnegation, at the same time as a surplus of cruelty and inhumanity; a surplus of dissidence at the outset and a surplus of bureaucracy at the end (in the best-case scenario, leaving aside camps, trials and executions). The double-edged character of a word blood red in colour, which connotes both a rising sun and an incendiary fantasy, has contributed not a little to its aura among several generations of activists or scapegoats.

This is not the place for an in-depth reflection on the value and limitations of a crucial term, which recent history has, as it were, temporarily laid off by restoring it to its original meaning, forlornly astronomical and bitterly cosmic, as the return of a star to the starting point of its orbit. Emancipation from an old order as heralding restoration of that self-same order did not feature in the dictionary of received ideas half a century ago. For now renouncing the indispensable task of the historian and philosopher, and sticking to the sensation of a writer, I must confess a certain hesitation at the belligerent tone, domineering and self-confident, of an ultimatum which, viewed from afar, is too much like a profession of faith. The lyrical illusion is perhaps not at its best when it forces itself to be didactic. But thus it was and there is no need to be embarrassed about it.

June 2017   RÉGIS DEBRAY,
                    TRANSLATED BY GREGORY ELLIOTT

FOREWORD

THE circumstances under which this work was written and the identity of its author are explained in the Introduction written for the original Spanish edition by Roberto Fernández Retamar and included in this English translation. It remains for us only to add information, useful to the reader, on developments since publication in Havana in January 1967.

To begin with, the size of the first printing (200,000 copies) and the evident eagerness of representatives of the Cuban regime to secure the widest distribution of the work both inside and outside Cuba leave no doubt that Régis Debray, though writing only in his capacity as a private student of revolutionary theory and practice, has succeeded in presenting to the world an accurate and profound account of the thinking of the leaders of the Cuban Revolution on these subjects. It is not to depreciate Debray's contribution to say that we have here for the first time a comprehensive and authoritative presentation of the revolutionary thought of Fidel Castro and Che Guevara.

That alone would be sufficient to mark the work as one of first importance. But there is an added reason. As the very title implies, we have to do not only with a work on revolutionary thought but one which aims to revolutionize revolutionary thought. As far as Latin America is concerned, Debray and the Cuban leaders believe, the revolution will not and cannot follow one or another of the patterns traced out by the two great revolutionary upheavals of the first half of the twentieth century. The Latin American revolution is taking a third way, the first stages of which have already been revealed in the Cuban experience. Hence the need amounting to a necessity for Latin American revolutionaries to study the

Cuban experience, to learn its lessons, and to guide their actions accordingly.

But it is not only Latin American revolutionaries who are concerned. If Debray is right, the 'Latin American way' may be of the utmost relevance to other countries around the world which are faced with conditions essentially similar to those of Latin America. And if a third way is possible, then those of us who live in countries where conditions are basically different from those obtaining in Tsarist Russia or Kuomintang China or contemporary Latin America, had better ask ourselves very seriously whether still other revolutionary patterns may not be possible. In short, this little work represents a very real challenge to all revolutionaries everywhere.

For this same reason it also represents a danger to the guardians of the status quo, and above all to the Latin American oligarchies and their North American boss and keeper. What has happened to Régis Debray since publication of his book shows that they are well aware of this. In April he went as a journalist and writer, accredited by the Mexican weekly *Sucesos* and by the Paris publishing house of Maspero, to report on the then newly opened guerrilla front in southern Bolivia. He was arrested by the Bolivian police, while travelling under his own name and in civilian clothes; and he has since been held incommunicado despite protests and representations from all over the world, including a letter from France's President de Gaulle to the Bolivian dictator. By way of answer, the latter has announced that Debray will be tried by a military court and faces a possible death sentence. Meanwhile reports – credible in view of what is known of present-day Latin American realities – have circulated that Debray has been tortured and starved in prison and that he has been subjected to lengthy interrogation by the United States Central Intelligence Agency.

Why such barbarous treatment for a mere journalist? We believe that Jean-Paul Sartre, the illustrious French philosopher, stated the simple truth when he told a mass meeting in Paris on 30 May (according to the report in *Le Monde*): 'Régis Debray has been arrested by the Bolivian authorities, not for having participated in guerrilla activities but for having written a book – *Révolution dans la révolution?* – which "removes all the brakes from guerrilla activities". '

The book presented difficult problems of translation. Debray's style tends to be both allusive and elliptical, and it shows the strong influence of his philosophical studies at the École Normale Supérieure. Just how great the difficulties were (and the sad consequences of not overcoming them) can be gauged by a brief perusal of the English translation of Debray's work put out by the United States government's Joint Publications Research Service (JPRS 40,310, 20 March 1967) which is not only completely unreliable but often grotesque in its errors and misunderstandings. In contrast, we believe that Bobbye Ortiz, translator of the present version, has done a remarkable job in producing an accurate and readable text. She worked from both the Spanish and French editions, each of which was prepared for the press by the author himself, and compared her results – without measurable assistance, it must be said – with the JPRS version throughout. It would of course have been desirable for the author to have had the opportunity to pass on the final draft; but for reasons with which the reader is already familiar from the account above, this was unfortunately not possible.

12 June 1967   LEO HUBERMAN
                                        PAUL M. SWEEZY

INTRODUCTION TO THE SPANISH EDITION

THE readers of our America became acquainted with Régis Debray through the publication of his essay 'América Latina: algunos problemas de estrategia revolucionaria' in the magazine *Casa de las Américas* (No. 31, July–August 1965). In January of the same year *Les Temps Modernes* had published 'Le castrisme: la longue marche de l'Amérique latine'. Republished several times, both works attracted a vast audience and soon made of their author, in his twenties, one of the most lucid interpreters of the current Latin American scene.

Debray had his first contact with the Cuban revolution in 1961, when he witnessed the gigantic literacy drive carried on during that year, which transformed Cuba into the first Latin American country free of illiteracy. The dazzling certainty of a reality which he had experienced crystallized in him an interest in the study of contemporary revolutionary phenomena, governed by Marxist thought. He has never shrunk from a confrontation with reality; his conceptions have their origins in reality, and they have the sense of immediacy and the necessary degree of passion which such an origin presupposes.

After Cuba, Debray travelled in several countries of the continent, making close contact with revolutionaries and on some occasions sharing the life of the *guerrilleros*. Thus he came to know Latin America not through preconceived ideas but through experience. A professor of philosophy – having studied with the great Marxist thinker, Louis Althusser – he continued, after his return to France, to draw lessons from his Latin American experience; the result was the above mentioned articles which can be looked upon as two parts of a single work. In them intellectual rigour is joined with direct knowledge of the subject under discussion.

At the end of 1965 Debray returned to Cuba, having resolved to deepen his understanding of the revolutionary experience. It was his view that up to then the subject had been insufficiently studied. The subtlety of his concepts, his great analytical ability, and the originality of his approach, already revealed in the earlier articles, awakened the interest of the leading circles of the Cuban Revolution who offered him every facility for carrying out his investigation. During 1966 he was able to speak with many who had participated in our revolutionary actions: among others, with Major Fidel Castro, who conceived and led that struggle. There were many long conversations, and Debray heard accounts of the experiences undergone, sometimes at the very site of decisive military actions. Furthermore, he had access to numerous unpublished documents of that epoch which had been preserved: messages written in combat, instructions to military leaders in the field, military communiqués, letters, and other texts. This gave him the opportunity to obtain a most vivid impression of those historic events. No one else who has written about the Cuban Revolution has had access to such a wealth of material for historical research.

Of course Debray has not written a history of that process, but he has drawn fundamental military and political conclusions from it, contrasting them with the personal experiences, the successes and the mistakes of other guerrilla movements which he knew directly, or about which he was able to obtain fresh and reliable information.

It is with great satisfaction that we inaugurate the *Cuadernos* series of *Casa de las Américas* with this essay, which, even more than the author's earlier essays, is bound to arouse the interest of those who, everywhere on the continent of Bolívar and Martí, of Fidel and Che, know that *the duty of a revolutionary is to make the revolution.*

ROBERTO FERNÁNDEZ RETAMAR

PREFACE

'The Cuban Revolution can no longer be repeated in Latin America.'

This phrase, on the lips of Latin American activists, has become a dangerous cliché. Although true in some respects, it has given rise to certain flagrant oversights.

By saying that the Cuban Revolution will not have an equivalent on the continent because the relationship of forces has changed, we calmly forget what it is that cannot be repeated; the A B Cs of the Cuban Revolution are ignored.

First, we reduce Cuba to a golden legend, that of twelve men who disembark and whose numbers multiply in the twinkling of an eye, no one knows quite how. Then we say that reality no longer has anything to do with this bold fairy tale. This conjuring trick has simply allowed the essential, the complex reality of the Cuban insurrectional process to be overlooked.

How many useless gyrations, how much lost time, how many unfortunate experiences have resulted for present-day revolutionary movements! I attempted in earlier studies to show the extent of the changes on the continent wrought by Cuba. But it is now necessary to take note of an inverse movement which is beginning among combatants and activists everywhere; they are returning to the Cuban experience with interest, seeking the 'how' of it rather than its surface glitter, its political and military 'details', and its inner workings. Why? Because after years of sacrifices, and at times of waste, they are discovering truths of a technical, tactical, and even of a strategic order which the Cuban Revolution had demonstrated and acted upon from its inception, though sometimes unconsciously. They are discovering that a certain way of loudly hailing the legend of the *fidelista* insurrection has concealed, even from themselves, a kind of disdain or refusal to learn from it and perceive its fundamental lessons.

Thus we cannot but deplore the continuing lack of a detailed history of the Cuban insurrectional process, a history which can come to us only from those who organized and participated in it. This lack constrains us to reduce our references to allusions, whereas what is really needed is a systematic investigation.

I

TO FREE THE PRESENT
FROM THE PAST

WE are never completely contemporaneous with our present. History advances in disguise; it appears on stage wearing the mask of the preceding scene, and we tend to lose the meaning of the play. Each time the curtain rises, continuity has to be re-established. The blame, of course, is not history's, but lies in our vision, encumbered with memory and images learned in the past. We see the past superimposed on the present, even when the present is a revolution.

The impact of the Cuban Revolution has been experienced and pondered, principally in Latin America, by methods and schemas already catalogued, enthroned, and consecrated by history. This is why, in spite of all the commotion it has provoked, the shock has been softened. Today the tumult has died down; Cuba's real significance and the scope of its lessons, which had been overlooked before, are being discovered. A new conception of guerrilla warfare is coming to light.

Among other things, Cuba remembered from the beginning that the socialist revolution is the result of an armed struggle against the armed power of the bourgeois state. This old historic law, of a strategic nature if you like, was at first given a known tactical content. One began by identifying the guerrilla struggle with insurrection because the archetype – 1917 – had taken this form, and because Lenin and later Stalin had developed several theoretical formulas based on it – formulas which have nothing to do with the present situation and which are periodically debated in vain, such as those which refer to conditions for the outbreak of an insurrection, meaning an immediate assault on the central power. But this disparity soon became evident. American

guerrilla warfare was next virtually identified with Asian
guerrilla warfare, since both are 'irregular' wars of encirclement of cities from the countryside. This confusion is even
more dangerous than the first.

The armed revolutionary struggle encounters specific conditions on each continent, in each country, but these are
neither 'natural' nor obvious. So true is this that in each
case years of sacrifice are necessary in order to discover and
acquire an awareness of them. The Russian Social Democrats instinctively thought in terms of repeating the Paris
Commune in Petrograd; the Chinese Communists in terms
of repeating the Russian October in the Canton of the twenties; and the Vietnamese comrades, a year after the foundation of their party, in terms of organizing insurrections of
peasant soviets in the northern part of their country. It is
now clear to us today that soviet-type insurrections could
not triumph in pre-war colonial Asia, but it was precisely
here that the most genuine Communist activists had to begin
their apprenticeship for victory.

One may well consider it a stroke of good luck that Fidel
had not read the military writings of Mao Tse-tung before dis-
embarking on the coast of Oriente: he could thus invent, on
the spot and out of his own experience, principles of a military doctrine in conformity with the terrain. It was only at
the end of the war, when their tactics were already defined,
that the rebels discovered the writings of Mao.* But once

* It is well known that Fidel drew his fundamental political inspiration
from Martí, an inspiration reinforced and rectified, even before Moncada,
by the ideas of Marx and Lenin. In regard to Lenin, Fidel was especially
interested in the ideas expressed in *State and Revolution*, in which the
destruction of the old state apparatus and its repressive instruments becomes a revolutionary axiom. But the sources of his military inspiration
were to be found elsewhere: *Realengo 18*, by Pablo de la Torriente Brau;
accounts of the campaigns of Máximo Gomez; Engels's texts explaining
the difficult conditions of street fighting imposed on the Parisian proletariat by the Chassepot [breech-loading rifle used by the French Army in the
1870s] and by the opening up of broad avenues; Hemingway's *For Whom
the Bell Tolls* (in which Pablo and his quasi-guerrilla band lived in
the Sierra in the very rearguard of the fascists, between Madrid and

again in Latin America, militants are reading Fidel's speeches
and Che Guevara's writings with eyes that have already read
Mao on the anti-Japanese war, Giap, and certain texts of
Lenin – and they think they recognize the latter in the
former. Classical visual superimposition, but dangerous,
since the Latin American revolutionary war possesses highly
special and profoundly distinct conditions of development,
which can only be discovered through a particular experience. In that sense all the theoretical works on people's war
do as much harm as good. They have been called the grammar
books of the war. But a foreign language is learned faster
in a country where it must be spoken than at home studying
a language manual. In time of war questions of speed are
vital, especially in the early stages when an unarmed and
inexperienced guerrilla band must confront a well-armed
and knowledgeable enemy.

Fidel once blamed certain failures of the guerrillas on a
purely intellectual attitude towards war. The reason is under-
standable: aside from his physical weakness and lack of ad-
justment to rural life, the intellectual will try to grasp the
present through preconceived ideological constructs and
live it through books. He will be less able than others to
invent, improvise, make do with available resources, decide
instantly on bold moves when he is in a tight spot. Thinking
that he already knows, he will learn more slowly, display less
flexibility. And the irony of history has willed, by virtue of
the social situation of many Latin American countries, the
assignment of precisely this vanguard role to students and
revolutionary intellectuals, who have had to unleash, or
rather initiate, the highest forms of class struggle.

Subsequently these errors – these misunderstandings –

Segovia). These books were not so much sources as they were coincid-
ences: Fidel found in them only what he was looking for. Mao Tse-tung's
Problems of Strategy in Guerrilla War Against Japan came into Fidel's and
Che's hands after the 1958 summer offensive: to their surprise they found
in this book what they had been practising under pressure of necessity.

have been paid for. At not too high a price if we compare with the disasters, repeated over so many years, in the first war of liberation from Spain. A reading of Bolívar's biography reveals an enormous amount about war and about America – including valid lessons for today's American revolutionary wars. The most valuable of these: tenacity. Five times expelled from American soil within four years, defeated, ridiculed, alone, and with an obstinacy characterized as insanity, five times he returned, and won his first victory at Boyacá. Each time he learned a little more: the need for mobility and for cavalry, so as to compensate for the lack of troops and arms; the need to wage an aggressive and fast, not a defensive and static, war; the need to burn ships and to cut off any possible retreat by declaring a 'war to the death' against the Spaniard, in order to hasten the formation of what we call today 'subjective conditions' among his own followers and among the *criollos* [American-born descendants of Spaniards]; the trap that Caracas constituted as long as the Spaniards controlled the countryside; the need to encircle the cities by attacking from the plains and from solidly defended bases; the importance, lastly, of certain places ('Coro is to Caracas what Caracas is to America').

We have recently been given the same lesson in tenacity by Fidel, more than once on the brink of disaster. Moncada (1953), the Granma landing (1956), and to a lesser extent the failure of the April 1958 strike are other reverses which would have led most men to go home and wait for better days. How many guerrilla *focos** foundered in Guatemala prior to the consolidation of the Zacapa and Izabal guerrilla bands? Quite a few, annihilated or dismantled. How many defeats in Venezuela, how many betrayals and splits? None the less, the guerrilla forces have survived and are beginning again, more

* The Spanish word *foco* (French *foyer*) refers to a centre of guerrilla operations rather than a military base in the usual sense. Since there is no exact English equivalent, the original Spanish word has been retained throughout. – Tr.

vigorously than ever; perhaps the war itself is really beginning in earnest.

The reverses suffered by the Latin American revolutionary movement are truly minor if one measures them in terms of the short period of time which is the prologue to the great struggles of tomorrow, if we take into account the fact that the few years which have passed correspond to that period of 'takeoff' and readjustment through which all revolutions must go in their early stages. Indeed, what seems surprising is that guerrilla movements have been able to survive so many false starts and so many errors, some inevitable and others not. According to Fidel, that is the astonishing thing, and it proves the extent to which the movement is impelled by history. In fact, we must speak not so much of defeat as of a certain explicable stagnation and lack of rapid development, the consequences of, among other things, the inevitable blunders and errors at this stage of exploration of revolutionary conceptions and methods which are *new*, in spite of their deceptive kinship with other international experiences.

All decisive revolutionary processes must begin and have begun with certain mis-steps for the reason that we have mentioned: because the existing points of departure are those left by the preceding historical period, and they are used, even if unconsciously. Of all these false starts, the Latin American is the most innocuous. In each case it has been a matter of adjusting the pace without changing the direction of movement, of correcting tactics without renouncing correct strategies or principles. At such a time profound differences between two camps come to the surface.

In each country that has experienced a revolution a confrontation has taken place between revolutionaries on one side and reformists and future renegades on the other. After 1905 pacifism and the defeatist spirit gained strength in the Russian Social Democratic Party. Lenin, in exile in Geneva, and others had to raise their voices, not to oppose the representative democracy of the Dumas to a workers' insurrection, but to oppose an undirected insurrection to a well-directed one. In China, after the 1927 defeats, it was necessary to oppose, as Mao and others did, a rapid uprising in the big cities under the domination of the Kuomintang enemy, not to a renewed commitment to workers' insurrection, but to a retreat to the countryside and the Long March – a form of struggle appropriate to Chinese conditions. After the Moncada disaster of 1953 Fidel and his surviving comrades did not consider abandoning the principle of armed struggle against Batista, but they gave it a different, more correct content. For a revolutionary, failure is a springboard. As a source of theory it is richer than victory: it accumulates experience and knowledge.

In Latin America a few years of experience in armed struggle of all kinds have done more to reveal the particularity of objective conditions than the preceding decades of borrowed political theory. Historically Cuba has established the point of departure of the armed revolution in Latin America. It is this point of departure, assiduously preserved and based on a correct line, which is essential.

Has the armed struggle really broken out? Are these its first fruits in Venezuela, Guatemala, Colombia, Peru, Ecuador? Or are they merely skirmishes, manifestations of a restlessness that has not yet borne fruit? The outcome of today's struggles is not important. As far as the final result is concerned it does not matter whether one movement or another is temporarily defeated.

What is decisive is the determination to struggle which is maturing daily, the awareness of the need for revolutionary change and the certainty of its possibility.*

In Latin America today a political line which, in terms of its consequences, is not susceptible to expression as a precise and consistent military line, cannot be considered revolution-

* Che Guevara, 'La guerre de guérilla, une méthode', in *Souvenirs de la guerre révolutionnaire*, Maspero, Paris 1967. (An English translation of this book is being prepared by Monthly Review Press. – Ed.)

ary. Any line that claims to be revolutionary must give a concrete answer to the question: How to overthrow the power of the capitalist state? In other words, how to break its backbone, the army, continuously reinforced by North American military missions? The Cuban Revolution offers an answer to fraternal Latin American countries which has still to be studied in its historical details: by means of the more or less slow building up, through guerrilla warfare carried out in suitably chosen rural zones, of a *mobile strategic force*, nucleus of a people's army and of a future socialist state.

Any military line depends on a political line which it expresses. It so happens that during the past few years other military lines have been tested within the armed struggle itself, giving an entirely different meaning to guerrilla warfare. More than poor interpretations of the Cuban answer, they are *imported* political conceptions, disguised as military lines and applied to historic conditions very different from those in which they had their roots. We have in mind: the concept of armed self-defence; a particular way of interpreting armed propaganda and the guerrilla base; and finally, the subjection of the guerrilla force to the party as just one more component added to its peacetime organization.

To judge by results, these conceptions which in many places have acquired the status of guiding policy lines, have emptied the popular armed struggle of much of its content. It is worthwhile investigating the political ideas which inspire them and the manner in which some have borrowed from revolutionary experiences alien to Latin America and its present-day conditions.

These negative experiences may help us to discover the essential lessons to be drawn both from the insurrectional phase of the Cuban Revolution and from today's armed struggles.

ARMED SELF-DEFENCE

TODAY self-defence as a system and as a reality has been liquidated by the march of events.

Colombia with its zones of peasant self-defence, and Bolivia with its zones of worker self-defence, constituted the two countries in which this conception acquired the strength of a line. These two 'nuclei of subversion' were, within a few months of each other, liquidated by the army: Marquetalia, in southern Colombia, occupied in May of 1964, and the Bolivian mines invaded in May and September of 1965, after tragic battles. This double defeat signifies the end of an epoch and attests to the death of a certain ideology. It is necessary that the revolutionary movement should once and for all accept this demise.

The end of an epoch, the epoch of relative class equilibrium. The beginning of another, that of total class warfare, excluding compromise solutions and shared power.

In view of the present polarization of exploited and exploiters in a neocolonial country, the fact that a portion of territory can exist in which the army and the state cannot proceed 'to the normal exercise of their functions', is more than the new imperialist legality can tolerate but at the same time not enough to endanger it. The failure of armed self-defence of the masses corresponds on the military level to the failure of reformism on the political level. In the new context of struggle to the death there is no place for spurious solutions, no place for the pursuit of an equilibrium between oligarchic and popular forces through tacit non-aggression pacts. Oligarchical dictatorships pose the alternative of beginning to destroy them *en bloc* or of accepting them *en bloc*: there is no middle way. Besides, self-defence is discredited today; its own former supporters have made of it the beginning of higher forms of struggle. But beware! It tends to appear again in more seductive forms, though naturally without revealing its name. It tends to reappear because it is rooted in an ideology with as many shapes as Proteus. At the time self-defence was foundering, Trotskyism came along to extend a hand to it and attempt to revive it. It is this rebirth that concerns us here.

In the ideological background of self-defence there are to be found ideologies which Lenin repeatedly described as indigenous to the working class and which he said would again and again come to the fore whenever Marxists and Communists lowered their guard: 'economism' and 'spontaneity'. Economism is the exclusive defence by trade unions of the workers' job interests against encroachments by the power of management. Since an *attack* on the bosses' political power – the bourgeois state – is excluded, such a defence in effect accepts and guarantees that which it claims to combat. It is not by mere chance that it is in Bolivia, where the oldest anarcho-syndicalist tradition among the workers exists, that the struggle has, since the 1952 revolution, taken the form of a workers' self-defence militia.

The term self-defence is not the most apt. It suggests a passive, timorous, withdrawn approach, but this is not always correct. In fact, it is rarely the case. Who would question the fighting heroism of the European proletarians before the 'importation of Marxism to the working class', according to Lenin's formula? And the courage and prowess in battle of the Colombian peasants, who were the principal victims of that terrible ten-year civil war in which more than 100,000 of them fell? Who would deny that the sacrifice and solidarity of the Paris workers during the 'June days' and the Commune are met again in 1952 in the 40,000 miners and industrial workers of La Paz, the heroes of the first American workers' revolution?

Self-defence does not suffer from a lack of boldness among its promoters. Quite to the contrary, it frequently suffers from a profusion of admirable sacrifices, of wasted heroism leading nowhere – that is, leading anywhere except to the conquest of political power. It is therefore better to speak of armed spontaneity. Its very ideological origin reveals to us the epoch in which it was born: prior to Marx. The Indian uprising led by Túpac Amaru II in Peru at the end of the eighteenth century could well have been called self-defence. The Indians rose up, by the tens of thousands, drove out the *criollo* landowners, killed the Spaniards on the spot, and recovered the land stolen from them by the *encomienda* system. The movement, however, was quickly dissipated in local victories; the Indians, as they approached the coast, occupied the lands and remained in the mountains: no more or less regular army, no independent shock troops. The insurgents, masters of the countryside, disdained to march on Lima, seat of the Vice Royalty. This gave Lima time to regroup an army; and reconquest was achieved without difficulty, under what conditions one can well imagine. The uprising of the *Comuneros* of Colombia, led by the famous Manuela Beltrán, in roughly the same epoch, could also be called self-defence.

In short, there were workers' insurrections before the advent of scientific socialism, as there were peasant wars before there were revolutionary guerrilla wars. But neither in the one case nor in the other is there an interrelation. Guerrilla warfare is to peasant uprisings what Marx is to Sorel.

Just as economism denies the vanguard role of the party, self-defence denies the role of the armed unit, which is organically separate from the civilian population. Just as reformism aims to constitute a mass party without selection of its militants or disciplined organization, self-defence aspires to integrate everyone into the armed struggle, to create a mass guerrilla force, with women, children, and domestic animals in the midst of the guerrilla column.

Just as spontaneity does not aspire to political power for the exploited and consequently does not organize itself into a political party, self-defence does not aim at military

supremacy for the exploited and consequently does not aspire
to organize itself as a popular regular army with its own
mobility and initiative. It may be said that there is self-
defence wherever a strategic mobile force is not the number
one objective of the armed struggle, wherever the conquest
of political power is not the conscious and visible goal. Self-
defence does not exclude insurrection, but such an insurrection will always be local and will not seek to extend its action
to the entire country. Self-defence is partial; revolutionary
guerrilla warfare aims at total war by combining under its
hegemony all forms of struggle at all points within the territory. Local, therefore localized from the beginning, the
community practising self-defence is denied any initiative.
There is no choice of the site of combat, no benefits of mobility, manoeuvre, or surprise. Since the zone of self-defence
is already exposed, it will be the object of an encircling action
and a carefully prepared attack by the enemy at the moment
of his own choosing. The zone or city defended by the
population itself can only passively await the enemy's attack
and is dependent on its goodwill. Nor does self-defence oblige
the enemy to 'see to it that the situation does not worsen'.
(Che Guevara.) It does not force either representative
democracies or oligarchic regimes to reveal their class content openly. Self-defence permits the ruling class to conceal
its true character as a dictatorship of violence; it maintains
the 'equilibrium between oligarchic dictatorship and popular pressure' rather than 'rupturing' it. (Che.) It enters into
and plays the game of the ruling class, promoting divisions
in the dominated classes, disguising compromise solutions as
victories.

In Vietnam above all, and also in China, armed self-
defence of the peasants, organized in militias, has played an
important role as the foundation stone of the structure of the
armed forces of liberation – but self-defence extended to zones
already militarily liberated or semi-liberated; in no way did
it bring autonomous zones into being. These territories of

self-defence were viable only because total war was being carried out on other fronts, with the regular and mobile forces of the Vietminh. They permitted the integration of the entire population into the war without resting the principal weight of the struggle upon it. By dispersing the French expeditionary force these zones lightened the task of the regular and semi-regular forces and permitted them to concentrate a maximum of troops on battle fronts chosen in accordance with the strategic plans of the General Staff. Even less than in Vietnam can self-defence be self-sufficing in Latin America – at least not if one aims to avoid the elimination of the civilian population.

Che Guevara writes, in his preface to Giap's *Guerre du peuple, armée du peuple*:

> Self-defence is nothing more than a small part of a whole, with special characteristics. It is never possible to conceive of a self-defence zone as complete in itself, i.e. as a region where the popular forces attempt to defend themselves against enemy attack, while the entire zone beyond remains free of disturbances. In such a case, the *foco* would be localized, cornered, and defeated, unless there occurred an immediate passage to the first phase of the people's war, in other words, to guerrilla warfare.

Some time after Che wrote this, 'the peasant zone of self-defence' of Marquetalia [Colombia] and the other 'independent republics' were occupied and dissolved by the enemy, and Marulanda had to return to mobile guerrilla warfare. A self-defence zone when it is neither the result of a total or partial military defeat of enemy forces, nor protected by a guerrilla front constantly on the offensive, is no more than a colossus with feet of clay. Its collapse deals a blow to the morale of the popular forces all the more serious and unexpected because this type of status quo appears to be unalterable; a euphoric mythology develops and envelops the reality of these zones. Since they may last for years, it is forgotten that they are the fruit of a tacit compromise, not of a real victory; and they come to be considered impregnable.

Vigilance is lulled; more and more it is forgotten to put the militias to the test, to supervise training and armament; discipline is relaxed. On the revolutionary side these territories, presumably liberated, are converted into a simple object of political propaganda – alibis for inaction rather than incitations to greater action. On the side of reaction they provide ready-made justification for posing as guardians of national unity and territorial integrity threatened by this cancerous growth, and for attacking the communist 'separatists'. For propaganda reasons the bourgeoisie little by little inflates the real danger and the fear it feels, an inflation which can deceive the revolutionaries themselves, eventually persuading them that the guerrilla force is really a cancer, and that time alone will finish off the patient. Thus, the 'subsiding of the swelling', when the army passes over to the attack after long preparations made at its leisure, will have a major effect: a great victory for the bourgeoisie, a great defeat for the 'Castro–Communist revolution'.

What is the reality?

If one judges by the history of Cuba and certain other Latin American countries, guerrilla warfare seems to pass through the following stages: first, the stage of establishment; second, the stage of development, marked by the enemy offensive carried out with all available means (operational and tactical encirclements, airborne troops, bombardments, etc.); finally, the stage of revolutionary offensive, at once political and military. During the first stage, clearly the hardest to surmount and the most exposed to all sorts of accidents, the initial group experiences at the outset a period of absolute nomadism; later, a longer period of hardening or seasoning by the combatants, the organization of a regular mail service, of supply lines, of relief forces, of arms depots, arriving at the final phase of the true establishment or minimal constitution of a zone of operations. This progression witnesses a growth in absolute numbers of fighters but also a relative diminution, since services, small-scale industry, and officer-cadres are developing: in other words, the technical side grows (armament, communications, production, explosives, training schools for recruits, etc.) in response to the development of guerrilla fire power and its offensive strength.

As it happens, a self-defence zone such as Marquetalia may give the impression of having reached the end of the first stage (consolidation of a zone of operations) and of being able to pass over immediately to the second: to face an enemy offensive, to take the tactical initiative, to detach units of the mother column in order to set up other guerrilla fronts. Not so. Since the territories of peasant self-defence were not the culmination of an armed revolutionary struggle, but of a civil war between conservatives and liberals – without a clear outcome, without effect on the enemy's military potential – the guerrilla bands, beginning with the Marquetalia group, had to return to the first phase, the nomadic phase, without ceasing to be burdened by the families of the combatants, the tasks of evacuating the population, care of cattle and farm implements, etc.

Bolivia: an analogous situation in a workers' milieu, takes on the aspects of tragedy. Twenty-six thousand miners in the big nationalized tin mines are spread over the entire *altiplano*, but the principal mining stronghold is concentrated in a belt of land some 9½ miles long by 6 wide, where the 'Siglo Veinte', 'Huanuni', and 'Catavi' mines are located. In 1952 the miners destroyed the oligarchy's army, established a liberal government, received arms and a semblance of power. The revolution turned bourgeois; the miners gradually severed connexions. They had arms, militias, radios, a strong union, dynamite and detonators – their everyday work tools – plus control of the country's basic wealth, tin – 'the devil's metal'. In retreat, semi-impotent, apathetic, they allowed the national bourgeoisie to reconstitute an army, and they interrupted their reign of strikes, skirmishes, and battles: in short, they were surviving. Then, as is natural, the army swallowed up the national bourgeoisie which had created it; and the order arrived from the United States to crush the workers' movement. The military junta provoked the workers in cold blood, arresting their old union leader Lechín. The unlimited general strike proposed by the Trotskyists was decreed in May 1965. The army's élite corps, the Rangers, special parachute troops, and the classic infantry surrounded the mines and unleashed a frontal attack against the miners' militia. Its aviation bombed a mine near La Paz and machine-gunned another. Result: hundreds of dead on the miners' side and dozens among the soldiers; occupation of the mines by the army; doors broken down by soldiers, and families machine-gunned indiscriminately; union leaders and the more militant miners outlawed, jailed, killed. Objective achieved. Everything in order, even the hatred and the tears of rage. Until the next time.

If there were a combined general insurrection at several mines, plus La Paz and certain rural areas, and if this insurrection brought to completion a long war of attrition carried on elsewhere by other means, miners organized in revolutionary unions could play a decisive role. But one thing appears to be impossible: that a spontaneous insurrection should be able, in a few days, to defeat a modern army, trained and reinforced by a well-equipped North American military mission, equipped with shock troops, few in number but aggressive. In short, times have changed; it would be difficult to repeat 1952 in 1966.

What possibility of defence and of victorious attack have the miners today?

The *milicianos* are workers in the nationalized mines. In the case of a strike or insurrection the government cuts off the roads and intercepts the food supply, which normally reaches the mining communities from La Paz by train and truck. In the mining district itself, at an altitude of over 12,000 feet, the rocky soil produces little. A few communities of Aymará Indians grow potatoes and cinchona, and they dry llama meat. From this subsistence economy comes nothing substantial. Therefore the comrades need a quick victory, since their food supply would be sufficient for only about ten days; after that, no milk for the children, no medical supplies in the hospitals, no meat at the butcher's. On the other hand, the miners can stop the shipping of ore by blocking the trains at the mine entrance. But it is an unequal fight and they are defeated at the outset. The government has money in the bank, North American loans at its disposal, commercial warehouses, access to a Chilean port; and they can hold out for a long time without the ore. The miner in arms is, with every day that passes, jeopardizing his family's food supply; the fate of one is the fate of the other. He sees his children waste away under his very eyes, his fellow workers stricken by silicosis, gasping and dying for lack of medicines – a mere few cough syrups. If they were alone, independent, in restricted units, a raid on the warehouses of neighbouring towns would suffice to supply them for several weeks. But as things are, hunger attacks both them and their families.

The mines are also cities, immense grey windowless barracks, located at some distance from the pits, where the families live. On a freezing highland plateau, with not a tree or a shrub, an expanse of red earth as far as the eye can see, an intense glare. The houses are laid out in rows, an easy and conspicuous target for the bombers. Bombardments threaten not production but population, since the mines are underground and surface installations few. The smelters are in England and the United States. Another weakness: the mines are ten or twenty or more miles apart. It is easy for the army to isolate them one by one, and difficult for the miners to get together to coordinate resistance: without a plan, without a centralized military command, without military training, without means of transport. Furthermore, the militia units can only move at night. At best, a few commandos can move by day against limited objectives, in the enemy's rearguard, towards the cities. But that kind of action goes beyond self-defence and beyond the concrete conditions of life of the *milicianos* who barely have time to eat – badly – and to sleep so as to continue working for an average wage of $30–$40 per month. Hence the impatience, the desperation; something must be done to break the blockade. But what? Without preparation, action is suicidal; dynamite thrown by hand is useless against a machine gun, and the rifles are Chaco War vintage. Bullets are expensive and scarce. And what can be done against planes? In order to destroy one army, another army is necessary, and this implies training, discipline, and arms. Fraternity and bravery do not make an army. Witness Spain, and the Paris Commune.

Bound to their place of work, together with the women who fight and the children; exposed to all kinds of reprisals against themselves and their kin; unable to manoeuvre or even to detach troops from their base in organized units; without military organization; without leadership or funds; in short, without the material possibility of turning themselves into a mobile force, the miners are simply condemned to slaughter. The army decides the day and hour of the massacre, where to begin the action, by what routes the columns of soldiers will move, where the paratroopers will land. The initiative and the secrecy of the preparations are left to the army; for the miners, nothing more than troop muster, with their own resources, in the full light of day. If their home base, already known, is attacked, it is easily liquidated. Their counter-attack, on the other hand, cannot go very far, since the nature of the terrain is such that it holds them and pulls them back like an elastic band.

Whether or not to provide the popular forces with an armed detachment, organically independent of the civilian population, freed from the tasks of civil defence, and with the goal of winning political power – such is the decisive criterion for distinguishing revolutionary phraseology from revolutionary theory. We know that Trotskyism flies in the face of common sense, in that its strength lies in its division. It is everywhere and nowhere. It exposes itself by hiding itself. It is never what it is – Trotskyist. The Trotskyist ideology has reappeared today from several directions, taking as its pretext several transitory defeats suffered by revolutionary action, but always proposing the same 'strategy for taking power'. Let us summarize it:

The worker and peasant masses everywhere crave social-ism, but they don't yet know it because they are still in the power of the Stalinist bureaucracies. Hence the latent spon-taneity of the workers must be awakened. For the attainment of this goal the guerrilla movement is not the highest form of revolutionary struggle; 'dual power' must be instituted at the base, that is, a call must be made for the formation of factory and peasant committees, the proliferation of which will ultimately permit the establishment of a single United Con-federation of Workers; this confederation, by means of in-stantaneous and generalized risings in the mountains and the cities, will be the instrument for taking power. From now on the work of agitation must aim at unleashing strikes and workers' demonstrations. In the countryside the aim should be the organization of peasant unions; occupation of the land; organization of localized insurrections, which will gradually spread to the cities, with the rallying cry of Socialist Revolution. The workers must, step by step, take control of the means of production. Then they must rise up immediately and directly against the state power, without intermediaries or specialized detachments. The Revolution will arise from existing or latent economic struggles, which will be sharp-ened to the point of becoming a mass insurrection – a direct passage from union action to insurrection.

Peru, Guatemala, and Brazil (São Paulo and the North-east) were the three countries chosen by the Latin American Bureau of Buenos Aires, section of the Fourth International. This was the way Hugo Blanco operated, on arrival from Argentina, with the peasants of Convención Valley; Julião's peasant leagues were to be manipulated in the same way;

and such until recently was the line imposed on Yon Sosa and the 13th of November Movement (MR-13) in Guatemala by Posadas's International which took advantage of MR-13's abandonment by and lack of assistance from other political organizations. *Revolución Socialista*, at one time the organ of MR-13, said in its first number (July 1964): 'The principle of organizing armed insurrection in stages, by way of a "people's war", is formal, bureaucratic, and militarist. It is based on the underestimation and using of the masses and the postponement of their direct intervention.'

Trotskyism attributes great importance to the socialist character of the revolution, to its future programme, and would like it to be judged by this purely phraseological question, as if declaring a thousand times that the revolution should be socialist would help call it into existence. But the nub of the question is not theoretical, it lies in the forms of organization through which the 'Socialist Revolution' will be realized. It is here that we discover not only that the revolution which they speak of is utopian, but that the means employed lead not to the revolution but to the scarcely utopian liquidation of existing popular movements. On this point, let us hear from the 'Edgar Ibarra' guerrilla front, a unit of the FAR (*Fuerzas Armadas Rebeldes*) of Guatemala, which, having demonstrated the inanity of a 'national democratic' programme for the Guatemalan revolution and the 'non-existence of the national bourgeoisie', addresses itself to the Trotskyist movement as follows:

This entire [Trotskyist] position leads, by means of a clever manoeuvre, to the removal of revolutionary content from the guerrilla movement; to the denial that it can become the army of the people; to the denial of the role of the peasantry in our countries' revolutionary wars; to the denial of the need for the military defeat of imperialism and its lackeys as a precondition to seizing power from them; to the concealment of the prolonged duration of the armed struggle; to the deceptive presentation of the insurrectional outlook as a short-term matter; to the splitting of the people's forces

and the diversion of revolutionary efforts into the peaceful organization of unions and mass organizations.*

Let us for the moment decide to take the Trotskyist conception seriously, and not as the pure and simple provocation
that it is in practice. We will observe a certain amount of
confusion. First, the imposition of the working-class model
of factory cells and proletarian trade unions on the peasant
reality (what is valid for a factory or capitalist metropolis is
valid for the Indian community, which dates back to Mayan
or Inca society); the underestimation, paradoxical after
such an imposition, of the role of the working class as the
leading force of the revolution; the confusing of armed
struggle – as a long process of building up a popular army
in the field – with a direct assault on power or a Bolshevik-
type insurrection in the city; a total incomprehension of the
relation of forces between the peasantry and the ruling class.
Whatever the theoretical confusions, and there are many,
one thing is certain: this beautiful verbal apparatus operates
in reality like a trap, and the trap shuts on the agricultural
workers and sometimes on the organizers as well. To pro-
mote public assemblies of the people in an Indian village,
or open union meetings, is simply to denounce the inhabitants to the forces of repression and the political cadres to the
police: it is to send them to prison or to their graves.

In the document from which we have already quoted, the
Guatemalan comrades write:

The slogan calling for occupation of the land and factories, which
could be helpful at certain stages of the struggle, provokes, when
used anarchically, massacres and tremendous setbacks for the
peasants and workers who do not yet have the strength to sustain
these invasions. The famous 'dispute' with the bourgeoisie over
the ownership of the means of production is inconceivable so long

* Summary of a letter sent by the 'Edgar Ibarra' guerrilla front to the
Central Committee of the PGT (Communist Party) and the national
leadership of MR-13 in October 1964, à propos the conflicts that had
arisen in the Guatemalan revolutionary movement.

as the ruling classes control the whole apparatus of repression. This tactic could be applied in zones where the development of guerrilla forces, or of the popular army, had proceeded to the point of being able to hold the wave of repression in check. Under other circumstances, it exposes the people's most vulnerable targets to the enemy's blows. Such actions can acquire the character of real provocations, causing defeats that oblige the people to retreat politically as the only way of protecting themselves against repression.

At bottom Trotskyism is a metaphysic paved with good intentions.* It is based on a belief in the natural goodness of the workers, which is always perverted by evil bureaucracies but never destroyed. There is a proletarian essence within peasants and workers alike which cannot be altered by circumstances. For them to become aware of it themselves, it is only necessary that they be given the word, that objectives be set for them which they see without seeing and which they know without knowing. Result: socialism becomes a reality, all at once, without delay, neat and tidy.

Because Trotskyism, in its final state of degeneration, is a medieval metaphysic, it is subject to the monotonies of its function. In space – everywhere the same: the same analyses and perspectives serve equally well for Peru and Belgium. In time – immutable: Trotskyism has nothing to learn from history. It already has the key to it: the proletariat, essentially wholesome and unfailingly socialist – eternally at odds, in its union activity, with the perverse formalism of the Stalinist bureaucracies. Prometheus struggling ceaselessly against a Zeus of a thousand disguises in order to steal from him the fire of liberation and keep it burning. Has anyone ever seen a concrete analysis of a concrete situation from the pen of a Trotskyist?

Condemned to exist in the present within the categories of the past, Trotskyism withers on the vine. Has it ever met with

* For a good description of the Trotskyist position, see Sartre: 'Les communistes et la paix'.

anything but defeat? The saboteurs of the revolution are everywhere. The contradiction lies in the fact that these guardians of the spontaneity of the masses – advocates of abandoning the rural proletariat to its fierce animosities, freed from that 'militarist' caste (the guerrillas descending on it from the cities) and finally left to its own devices – are frequently militants from neighbouring countries or from abroad. And they come not to participate in a liberation movement nor to serve it, but to lead and control it by using its weaknesses, which is a different matter. Strange spontaneity: it is not born on the spot, it is imported. But why be surprised? An abstract metaphysic, a concept with no grasp of history – general or specific – the Trotskyist ideology can only be applied from outside. Since it is not appropriate anywhere, it must be applied by force everywhere.*

Thus we see that in reality guerrilla warfare is, paradoxically, interpreted both by the proponents of reformist self-defence and by ultra-revolutionary Trotskyism as a militarist tendency towards isolation from the masses. The Trotskyist conception of insurrection resembles self-defence: both provocative, both acting in the name of the masses against the apparatuses, in the name of the action of the masses against the action of a 'handful of adventurers'. The masses are the scapegoats. These fine theoreticians lead them to suicide, singing hymns to their glory.

The proponents of self-defence (in practice) and the Trotskyists (in practice and theory) consider the trade union to be the organizational base and the motive force of the

* All of which does not justify either the decrees or the tabu that still conceal from some people the works of Trotsky, of whom Lenin said, shortly before he died, that he was 'distinguished not only by his exceptional abilities – personally he is, to be sure, the most able man in the present Central Committee – but also by his too far-reaching self-confidence and a disposition to be too much attracted by the purely administrative side of affairs.' (The quotation is from Lenin's so-called 'testament' which is reproduced in full in E. H. Carr, *A History of Soviet Russia: The Interregnum, 1923–1924*, New York and London, 1954, pp. 258–9, 263. – Ed.)

class struggle. Herein lies the explanation of a surprising coincidence. We have been told that Trotskyists are ultra-leftists. Nothing is farther from the truth. Trotskyism and reformism join in condemning guerrilla warfare, in hampering or sabotaging it.* It is no mere accident that these two movements have taken the Cuban Revolution as a target for their attacks in Latin America as well as in the rest of the world. This also explains why the new guerrilla movements that are asserting themselves so forcefully, such as the FALN in Venezuela under the command of Douglas Bravo, and the FAR in Guatemala, have had to fight on two fronts. The programmatic letter of the FAR, which we have cited above, is addressed to both the *Partido Guatemalteco de Trabajo* (Communist), before its transformation, and to Yon Sosa's MR-13, dominated at that time by the Trotskyists. It was on the basis of this remarkable formulation of the form and content of the Guatemalan Revolution that the new *Fuerzas Armadas Revolucionarias* were organized, late in 1965, by agreement with the renewed and rejuvenated *Partido Guatemalteco de Trabajo.*

What does experience up to now teach us?

The revolutionary guerrilla force is clandestine. It is born and develops secretly. The fighters themselves use pseudonyms. At the beginning they keep out of sight, and when they allow themselves to be seen it is at a time and place chosen by their chief. The guerrilla force is independent of the civilian population, in action as well as in military organization; consequently it need not assume the direct defence of

* It is useful to compare Henri Edmé's article in *Les Temps Modernes* (April 1966) with the one by Pumaruna [*Cuadernos de Ruedo Ibérico*, Paris, April–May 1966 – Tr.], leader of *Vanguardia Revolucionaria*, a Peruvian organization, remotely Trotskyist in origin. Edmé, whose premises are stated with considerable acuity, expresses the point of view of the more traditional Communist Parties. (See Osvaldo Barreto's answer in a forthcoming issue of *Casa de las Américas*.) The two authors reach analogous conclusions, vague as they are: localized peasant self-defence in the countryside, the organization of cadres and 'advanced' political struggles in the city.

the peasant population. The protection of the population depends on the progressive destruction of the enemy's military potential. It is relative to the overall balance of forces: the populace will be completely safe when the opposing forces are completely defeated. If the principal objective of a revolutionary guerrilla force is the destruction of the enemy's military potential, it cannot wait for the enemy to approach before taking the initiative and going over to the attack. In every case this objective requires that the guerrilla *foco* be independent of the families residing within the zone of operations.

First, to protect the population against the repressive army. Faced with elusive *guerrilleros*, the army takes vengeance on the peasants whom it suspects of being in contact with them. If it finds one among them who has withheld information it will kill him, declaring in its report to headquarters that he was a *guerrillero*, in this way giving evidence of its own heroism. Mobility, the special advantage of guerrilla forces over the civilian population, imposes a special responsibility on them with respect to the peasants, who are exposed day and night to repressive measures – eternal victims-by-substitution. The guerrilla force is thus clandestine for two reasons; it is concerned as much with the peasants' safety as with that of its own fighters. After all, the safety of the one is the safety of the other.

The *guerrilleros* avoid going to the villages and openly staying in a given house or on the land of a given family. If they do enter a village they may stop at all houses, so as to compromise all equally and not point a finger at a particular one who is helping them; or they will not stop at any. If they must hold a meeting, they pretend to assemble the population by force, so that if threatened with repression the people can claim they were coerced. Contacts are made out of town, secretly, and of course at a distance from the guerrilla encampment, utilizing intermediaries (persons or objects) if necessary. Informants and collaborators are not known to each other. In the guerrilla group itself, only a few leaders know the network of contacts. A 'hot' collaborator of the region who asks to be integrated into the guerrilla force is admitted without question, even if he arrives without a weapon, etc.

Second, to protect the safety of the guerrilla force itself: 'Constant vigilance, constant mistrust, constant mobility' – the three golden rules. All three are concerned with security. Various considerations of common sense necessitate wariness towards the civilian population and the maintenance of a certain aloofness. By their very situation civilians are exposed to repression and the constant presence and pressure of the enemy, who will attempt to buy them, corrupt them, or to extort from them by violence what cannot be bought. Not having undergone a process of selection or technical training, as have the guerrilla fighters, the civilians in a given zone of operations are more vulnerable to infiltration or moral corruption by the enemy. Therefore peasants, even those who collaborate with the guerrillas, are generally not permitted to go to the encampments, nor are they informed of the whereabouts of arms dumps, or of the destination or real objectives of the guerrilla patrols whose passage they may observe. 'We hid our intentions from the peasants,' Che relates, 'and if one of them passed near the scene of an ambush, we held him until the operation was completed.'* This vigilance does not necessarily imply mistrust: a peasant may easily commit an indiscretion and, even more easily, be subjected to torture. It is known that this vigilance is exercised vis-à-vis guides especially, all of whom are carefully misinformed concerning where the *guerrilleros* came from, where they are eventually going, etc.†

* *Souvenirs de la guerre révolutionnaire.*
† Eutimio Guerra, a simple peasant and the first guide of the rebels in the Sierra, who enjoyed their complete confidence, had received 10,000 pesos from Casillas to kill Fidel. By chance and, according to Fidel, 'a sixth sense', he was discovered and executed in time. What should one

Hence the necessity for moving the encampment immediately after anyone leaves it. If it is a *guerrillero* carrying a
message, he will know the terrain thoroughly and will thus
be able, on his return, to rejoin the moving column or to find
the new camp site. It has been observed more than once that
the man – *guerrillero* or peasant – who by virtue of his functions must go back and forth between the mountains and the
city, to carry messages or to gather information or make
contacts, is especially exposed to enemy action. It is through
him that attempts are made to infiltrate the guerrilla unit,
willingly or by force; it is thanks to him that it is possible to
discover the whereabouts of the fighters of a given *foco*.*

According to Fidel, the danger represented by this function of liaison between the guerrilla unit and the plains is of
a psychological order. At the outset the young combatant,
still uncertain of the possibilities of a guerrilla victory, leaves
the camp to fulfil his mission. There below, he discovers the
strength and ostentation of the encircling army, its equip-
ment and manpower. Then he remembers the hungry band
he has just left. The contrast is too great, the task seems unrealizable, and he loses faith in victory. He thinks it ridiculous or unreasonable to attempt to defeat so many soldiers,
with so many trucks and helicopters, with all manner of
arms and supplies. Sceptical, from then on he is at the mercy

---

expect today, when the enemy knows the irreplaceable value of a leader,
especially in the first stage? It was the treachery of a guide that led to
the assassination of Luis de la Puente in Peru.

* In July 1963 an entire guerrilla *foco* – 21 men – in the Izabal zone
of Guatemala was liquidated due to lack of vigilance. A guerrilla messenger was picked up in the city and forced, at the point of a machine-gun, to
lead a detachment of the Central American army to the camp. The
messenger leading the column took the most difficult path, thinking it
to be guarded by a sentry. He revealed his presence by a shout before
reaching the place where he expected to find the sentry. No one answered.
The messenger was killed, and the detachment entered the encampment
in the dead of night. The sentry had been relieved earlier in the evening,
because this access was considered to be impenetrable.

of the enemy. This is how it is with novices. The plain demoralizes and disorganizes the weak ones.

To sum up, the advantages a guerrilla force has over the repressive army can be utilized only if it can maintain and preserve its mobility and its flexibility. The carrying out of any operation, the secrecy surrounding preparations, the rapidity of execution, the element of surprise, all require extreme care. Only at the risk of losing initiative, speed of movement, and manoeuvrability, can a guerrilla unit take with it women, children, and household belongings from one village to another. To combine the exodus of civilians with guerrilla marches, frequently forced, is to deprive the guerrilla force of all offensive potential; it cannot even effectively defend the civilian population for which it has assumed responsibility. By restricting itself to the task of protecting civilians or passive self-defence, the guerrilla unit ceases to be the vanguard of the people as a whole and deprives itself of a national perspective. By going over to the counter-attack, on the other hand, it catalyses the people's energy and transforms the *foco* into a pole of attraction for the whole country.

Thus, self-defence reduces the guerrilla force to an exclusively tactical role and deprives it of the possibility of making even the slightest strategic revolutionary contribution. By choosing to operate at this level, it may be able to provide protection for the population for a limited time. But in the long run the opposite is true: self-defence undermines the security of the civilian population.

Allowing oneself to be attacked or limiting oneself to passive defence is to place oneself in the position of being unable to protect the population and to expose one's own forces to attrition. On the other hand, to seek for ways to attack the enemy is to put him on the permanent defensive, to exhaust him and prevent him from expanding his activities, to wrest the initiative from him, and to impede his search operations. Here we have the best way to fulfil our glorious mission of protecting the population.

These directives were addressed to the Vietminh fighters in their war of liberation against the French colonialists. They are even more valid for many Latin American countries today.

ARMED PROPAGANDA

THE guerrilla struggle has political motives and goals. It must have the support of the masses or disappear; before enlisting them directly, it must convince them that there are valid reasons for its existence so that the 'rebellion' will truly be – by the manner of its recruitment and the origins of its fighters – a 'war of the people'. In order to convince the masses, it is necessary to address them, that is, to address speeches, proclamations, explanations to them – in brief, to carry on political work, 'mass work'. Hence the first nucleus of fighters will be divided into small propaganda patrols which will cover the mountain areas, going into villages, holding meetings, speaking here and there, in order to explain the social goals of the Revolution, to denounce the enemies of the peasantry, to promise agrarian reform and punishment for traitors, etc. If the peasants are sceptical, their confidence in themselves must be restored by imbuing them with revolutionary faith; faith in the revolutionaries who are speaking to them. Cells, public or underground, will be organized in the villages; union struggles will be supported or initiated; and the programme of the Revolution will be reiterated again and again. It is only at the end of this stage, having achieved active support by the masses, a solid rearguard, regular provisioning, a broad intelligence network, rapid mail service, and a recruiting centre, that the guerrillas can pass over to direct action against the enemy.

Such, it seems, is the line of *armed propaganda*.

This conception is supported by unquestionable international experience.

In Vietnam, armed propaganda, linked directly to the organization of rural self-defence groups, seems to have played a decisive role in the course of the war of liberation against the French, especially during the formation of the people's regular army from 1940 to 1945.

As they proceeded from guerrilla warfare to a war of manoeuvre and then to attacks on fortified positions, the Vietnamese comrades gradually advanced from section to battalion or regiment, then to division, a progression not as natural as it might seem since it does not, for example, correspond to the line of progression of the revolutionary war in China, which from the outset saw regular armies in battle. Thus in Vietnam the Communist Party was the organizational nucleus from which and around which the people's army developed. In order to give substance and shape to the liberation army, the Party in 1944 created the 'Propaganda Section of the Liberation Army'. In this way the Party organized a nucleus of revolutionary cadres – such was the propaganda squad of the Party, led from the beginning by Giap. Subsequently this nucleus spread throughout the country to form people's militias and irregular guerrilla units. Its goal was not to fight but to establish fighting units.

Thus began the building *from the base up* of the Vietnamese Armed Liberation Forces, with three types of formations: paramilitary or guerrilla, regional, and regular. At the level of the village and district, guerrillas; at the level of the regions or 'interzone' (several provinces), interzonal or semi-regular units; finally, the principal army or mobile strategic force, without a fixed base or specified area of operations. The best of the guerrillas move into the interzonal force, and the best of the latter move into the regular army. Each layer of the pyramid rests on a lower layer but without crushing it. Each has its own function. The organization and dovetailing of these three forces from the bottom up is insured by the people, organized at the village level. The regular army – the spearhead – is welded to the base but maintains its autonomy of movement. As General Giap explains, the strategy of war against the French Expeditionary Force rested on the Party's ability to put these three forces into action, sometimes alternately, sometimes simultaneously. The guerrilla forces and the interzonal units disperse the enemy's expeditionary force in a territory too big for it, and immobilize it by harassment. Quantitatively the enemy's manoeuvrability is thus reduced to the minimum; its rearguard is never secure. Either it is everywhere and no longer has a concentrated shock force available to it, or it makes a stand at a single point leaving the rest of the country disarmed. 'If the enemy is concentrated, it loses ground; if it is scattered, it loses strength.' Yesterday the French were prisoners of this dilemma, today the North Americans.

It is an incontrovertible law that a regular army is defeated when its elite corps is destroyed. It is therefore the function of the guerrilla forces, acting in coordination with the campaign plans of the popular elite corps, to isolate and whittle down the enemy's elite corps. When the French shock troops – 16,000 men – were wiped out at Dienbienphu, the rest of the expeditionary force, immobilized by the popular militia throughout the Tonkin Bay area, was decapitated.

Thus in order to destroy the repressive shock force the people's side needs a shock force of its own; the confrontation of the two joins the regular armies in combat, but there remains this difference: the people's regular army relies at all times on the population as a whole (recruitment, supplies, transport, intelligence); if this support were lacking, not even one battle could be sustained.

The Armed Forces of Liberation in South Vietnam today have at their disposal a liberation army in the strictest sense of the word, as well as regional troops, and lastly a militia still termed a guerrilla force. But women, children, and old people cannot join the armed struggle directly. How, then, to mobilize them? By integrating them into production, sabotage, intelligence, transport, etc. This integration requires in turn the formation and organization of a political army, which acts as a protective covering for the army proper. In this way the political struggle serves as apprenticeship or training for the armed struggle. It is the form of struggle proper to the rearguard, important for carrying out mobilization and strengthening morale. In brief, political struggle and armed struggle go hand in hand; where one is weak, so is the other.

If in a country such as Vietnam armed propaganda has been the order of the day, the explanation is in the many propitious conditions that prevail. Very schematically, the following conditions can be suggested:

1. The high density of the peasant population, the over-population of the villages and towns, and the marked predominance of the peasantry over the urban population permit revolutionary propagandists to mingle easily with the people, 'like fish in water'. It was the same in China. Such propagandists pass all the more unobserved because the enemy is an occupier, a regular soldier, alien to village life and the customs of the country, and it is easy to divert his attention, whether it is the French or the Yankees in Vietnam or the Japanese in China. The numerical disproportion between the forces of the occupier and the populace does not permit control of the entire territory by the expeditionary force, whose network of surveillance leaves many gaps and hence an open field.

2. The propagandists are linked either with the bases of revolutionary support or with a people's army capable of backing them up or protecting them in their activities. Most important, they attest to the tangible and visible reality of military victories. Village meetings and assemblies have a pragmatic and serious content – no empty, programmatic lectures, no 'fine words' of the kind the peasants so justly fear, but appeals to join up with or give support to *existing* combat

units. The propagandists are supported by a real struggle. The war provides the *objective* daily milieu in which the peasants live. And not against just any enemy, but against a foreign, invading enemy, speaking a foreign language and living in the cities as an occupying force, too recently settled in the country to have acquired a natural prestige disguising its true character. Intellectually it is not difficult to call the invader's power into question, resting as it does on brute force, the right of conquest, a chance treaty among distant foreign powers, rather than on national customs, peculiarities, or traditions. Vietnamese armed propaganda has thus developed within the framework of a war of national liberation, of a real war, being carried out everywhere and in all ways, by an established regular army against a foreign enemy, entrenched at certain – and in some cases, fortified – points within the national territory.

Differences between Vietnam and Latin America lead to the following contrast: Whereas in Vietnam the military pyramid of the liberation forces is built from the base up, in Latin America on the other hand, it tends to be built from the apex down – the permanent forces first (the *foco*), then the semi-regular forces in the vicinity of the *foco*, and lastly or after victory (Cuba) the militia.

What is the situation in many Latin American countries today?

1. The guerrilla *focos*, when they first begin their activity, are located in regions of highly dispersed and relatively sparse population. Nobody, no new arrival, goes unnoticed in an Andean village, for example. Above all else, a stranger inspires distrust. The Quechua or Cakchiquel (Mayan) peasants have good reason to distrust the 'outsider', 'the white man'. They know very well that fine words cannot be eaten and will not protect them from bombardment. The poor peasant believes, first of all, in anyone who has a certain power, beginning with the power to do what he says. The system of oppression is subtle: it has existed from time

immemorial, fixed, entrenched, and solid. The army, the *guardia rural*, the *latifundista*'s private police, or nowadays the 'Green Berets' and Rangers, enjoy a prestige all the greater for being subconscious. This prestige constitutes the principal form of oppression: it immobilizes the discontented, silences them, leads them to swallow affronts at the mere sight of a uniform. The neocolonial ideal is still to show force in order not to have to use it, but to show it is in effect to use it.

In other words, the physical force of the police and army is considered to be unassailable, and unassailability cannot be challenged by words but by showing that a soldier and a policeman are no more bullet-proof than anyone else. The *guerrillero*, on the other hand, must use his strength in order to show it, since he has little to show but his determination and his ability to make use of his limited resources. He must make a show of strength and at the same time demonstrate that the enemy's strength is first and foremost his *bluster*. In order to destroy the idea of unassailability – that age-old accumulation of fear and humility vis-à-vis the *patrono*, the policeman, the *guardia rural* – there is nothing better than combat. Then, as Fidel tells us, the unassailability vanishes as rapidly as respect engendered by habit turns into ridicule. The very peasants who take up arms and join the guerrilla force on the same footing as the veterans begin to under-estimate the enemy and take him lightly; at this stage a con-trary duty devolves upon the guerrilla leadership: to concede some prestige to the enemy, so as to preclude the running of unnecessary risks.

2. The occupation and control of rural areas by reaction or directly by imperialism, their vigilance today greatly increased, should rid a given group of armed propagan-dists of all hope of remaining unnoticed, 'like fish in water'. The armed unit and the people's vanguard are not dealing with a foreign expeditionary force, with limited manpower, but with a well-established system of local domination. They

themselves are the foreigners, lacking status, who at the beginning can offer the populace nothing but bloodshed and pain. Furthermore, channels of communication are increasing; airports and landing fields are being built in the most remote areas, heretofore inaccessible by land routes.

On the other side of the Andes, for example, between the mountains and the Amazon basin, there is the famous highway that is meant to skirt the jungle and link up the tropical zones of Venezuela, Colombia, Peru, and Bolivia, as well as join each with its respective capital. As for North American imperialism, it has increased its forces in the field and is making every effort to present itself, not in repressive guise but in the shape of social and technical assistance: we are familiar with all the sociological projects now under way, staffed with international personnel, under an academic cover or depending directly on the OAS, whose assignment is to 'photograph' the social, economic, and individual situations of each family in the 'danger areas'. The OAS's *Plan 208* in Bolivia; *Simpático* in Colombia; *JOB 430* in Argentina; *Camelot* in Chile; *Colony* in Peru, etc. Thousands of Peace Corpsmen have succeeded in integrating themselves in rural areas – some of them by dint of hard work, patience, and at times real sacrifice – where they profit by the lack of political work by left-wing organizations. Even the most remote regions are today teeming with Catholic, Evangelical, Methodist, and Seventh-Day Adventist missionaries. In a word, all these close-knit networks of control strengthen the national machinery of domination. Without exaggerating the depth or scope of their penetration, we can say that they have indeed changed the scene.

3. Lastly, the absence of organized regular or semi-regular revolutionary forces. Armed propaganda, at least if it is geared to combat, seeks precisely to organize regular units or to expand existing units, by means of 'political recruiting'. Thus, villages are 'stormed' to assemble the populace and hold propaganda meetings. But in reality how have the in-

habitants of these villages been helped to rid themselves of their class enemies? In the course of these operations, few arms have been acquired. Even if young peasants are spurred by enthusiasm to join the *guerrilleros*, with what will they be armed?

Many comrades have concluded from these experiences that an ambush of a column of reinforcements or some other blow levelled at the enemy in the vicinity would have aroused more enthusiasm in a given village, attracted new recruits, given a more profound moral and political lesson to the villagers, and – most important of all – would have procured the arms so essential to a new guerrilla unit. The destruction of a troop transport truck or the public execution of a police torturer is more effective propaganda for the local population than a hundred speeches. Such conduct convinces them of the essential: that the Revolution is on the march, that the enemy is no longer invulnerable. It convinces them, to begin with, that the soldier is an enemy – their enemy – and that a war is under way, the progress of which is dependent on their daily activities. Afterwards, speeches may be made and will be heeded. In the process of such raids the fighters collect arms, reduce the enemy's military potential, acquire experience, demoralize enemy troops, and renew the hopes of militants throughout the country. The agitational and propagandistic impact resides in this very concentration of effects. A significant detail: During two years of warfare, Fidel did not hold a single political rally in his zone of operations.

The forms of military organization imposed by armed propaganda appear to have led to a certain inactivity or vacillation. Paradoxically, no guerrilla movement that has adopted such a concept of struggle has been able to extend its sphere of influence decisively. Indeed, in order to carry on armed agitation throughout an extended zone, the initial *foco* must divide its meagre forces into patrols, composed of a few men – from three to ten – so as to cover the greatest number of villages. A certain tactical advantage results: a broader area is covered; there is no need to exhaust local food supplies and other resources, thereby becoming a burden on the peasants; the effectiveness and numerical strength of the *foco* can be enhanced in the minds of the workers by a simple allusion to the other patrols in the area; most important of all, the *foco* cannot be captured or even located by the enemy who is thus thwarted in his efforts to encircle the guerrilla force as a whole. But, though mobility is gained, this has little effect on the military picture, since each patrol's firepower is insignificant. Thus, even if the command favours the highly theoretical mechanisms of 'concentration–dispersion', this system has only a paper existence during the early stages of a guerrilla force – lacking control or knowledge of the terrain, subjected to the hazards of jungle living, great distances, and difficult communications. Thus, dispersed in patrols too small for territories too large (5,000 square kilometres at a minimum), the relation of forces is unfavourable and will tend to become increasingly so. *The guerrilla forces are weak everywhere and the enemy, however scattered he may be, is strong everywhere.* Distributing the troops in patrols impedes the *formation of columns*, containing specialized units, rearguard and vanguard units, heavy weapons serviced by trained groups, small-unit mess facilities which lighten the logistic load. To use the Chinese metaphor, the guerrilla force, instead of closing up like a fist in order to strike at the enemy and tear off one of his fingers, opens up and spreads its own five fingers; and then it is the enemy that has the strength of a fist against each of the fingers. In this regard, purely intellectual conviction is not enough. Certain guerrilla movements were familiar with and had regularly read theoretical works rich in such metaphors; in spite of this they continued, until recently, to scatter their forces to an extreme.

If on the one hand the guerrilla force assures its own survival, it also assures that of the enemy; and it would be naïve to think that the relation of forces must necessarily change to its advantage. As the experience in Lara, Venezuela, has demonstrated – and, to some extent, that of Guatemala – political conflicts are magnified within the guerrilla movement, leading to a host of defections, personal disputes, and frictions arising from prolonged and unbearable inactivity. Conflicts with outside political forces – parties or organizations – arise and are intensified. Such forces, far from being convinced and won over by the guerrillas' experience and enthusiasm, see their suspicions confirmed in regard to this form of people's struggle; they give voice to their formerly silent disapproval and begin to discuss it openly. These rifts in turn further weaken the guerrilla force which, having won no significant military victories, has failed to grow. Meanwhile the enemy, profiting by the quarrels within the movement, corrupts, wins over, or buys off the weakest members and physically liquidates others.

Does this mean that armed propaganda or agitational activities should be rejected? No.

To judge from certain successful experiences, a guerrilla unit leaves something – or at least someone – behind it, in the course of its advance, behind its own lines if such exist, for the purpose of organizing what is to become a base of solid support. But in such a case the physical security of the populace is assured by regular forces, capable of repulsing the enemy. The base thus begins to organize itself as the embryo of the people's state. The work of agitation and propaganda – the effort to explain the new organization to the populace and to bring about the transfer of zonal administration to mass organizations – becomes fundamental, and future combats depend on it. Propaganda then attests to the liberating nature of combat and instils this message in the minds of the masses. Furthermore, it facilitates the organization of production, the collection of taxes, the interpretation of revolutionary laws, the maintenance of discipline, the creation of schools for cadres and for others, the digging of trenches and shelters for the protection of the civilian population against bombardments, etc. We can see that no present Latin American guerrilla movements have reached the stage where these activities are on the order of the day.

In other words, armed propaganda follows military action but does not precede it. Armed propaganda has more to do with the internal than with the external guerrilla front. The main point is that under present conditions the most important form of propaganda is successful military action.

To consider armed propaganda as a stage distinct from and prior to military operations is, it seems, to provoke the enemy needlessly, to expose the comrades working as propagandists to assassination or the need to escape, and to expose a future or possible zone of guerrilla action. Given the social, ideological, and psychological conditions of the peasantry in the majority of Latin America countries, given the divers intelligence agencies at the enemy's disposal (strongly reinforced since the Cuban Revolution), an agitational group, whether armed or not, will be watched, uncovered, and liquidated; in embryo if necessary. What is worse, its contacts, the cells it has organized, the people who have 'worked' in the rural areas, in the villages, and in the neighbouring towns will perhaps meet the same fate. If the enemy is astute enough to wait, he will not make a move until operations have begun or until even later, so as to permit his espionage services to infiltrate. A 'peasant' will be planted in the organization: the whereabouts of the entire guerrilla group will thus be known from the beginning and promptly liquidated.

What is the origin of this concept which reduces the *guerrillero* to a mere armed agitator?

The lack of previous experience in armed struggle under historic and social conditions peculiar to Latin America has made for imitation (perhaps unconscious) of the Vietnamese experience, torn from its context. A misreading of the Cuban Revolution – a revolution well known in its external detail but whose inner content has not yet been sufficiently studied – may also have played its part. It was perhaps wrong to link the name of *foco* with a people's army in the process of formation in the countryside, whose aim was the encirclement and arousal of the city population. A kind of biological interpretation has spontaneously tied the idea of a *foco* to that of contagion, of spontaneous generation, microbial spread to neighbouring tissue, by the simple magic effect of contact or proximity. A hundred men incite the mountain population with speeches; the régime, terrified, collapses to the accompaniment of jeers; and the *barbudos* are acclaimed by the people. In this way one confuses a military *foco* – motor force of a total war – with a *foco* of political agitation. It appears to have been simply forgotten that the '26th of July' Cubans first made a war without a single unilateral truce; that during only a few months of 1958, the Rebel Army engaged in more battles than have other American fronts during a year or two; that in two months the rebels broke Batista's last offensive; and that 300 *guerrilleros* repulsed and routed 10,000 men. A general counter-offensive followed.

This was a war that cost dearly in combatant casualties; a war that, although exceptionally short, required nonetheless a wealth of tactical inventiveness, mobility, and audacity, together with real soundness of strategy. It has simply been forgotten that *Patria o Muerte* is not a slogan with which to end speeches but a principle of conduct which the Cuban fighters followed to the letter in all their actions, from the attack on the small La Plata fort to the capture of Santa Clara. Strategically they staked all and in the end they won all.

Of course, this strategic decision – to stake everything – should not lead the guerrilla forces to a tactic of undertaking decisive battles that can cost them the revolution. The concept of an Ayacucho* has no place in a revolution of today; it is pointless to expect to win everything in one battle. In the

---

* The battle of Ayacucho in 1824 signified a decisive military victory for Sucre, Bolívar, and the Latin American independence fighters in the war against Spain. – Tr.

battle of Guisa, for example, in November 1958, Fidel, with 200 *guerrilleros* (of whom 100 were raw recruits), opposed 5,000 soldiers of the dictatorship, plus their tanks, planes, and artillery; but the rebels always had the possibility of withdrawing from the plain to the mountains, where they could skilfully take advantage of the terrain. The battle was more important for the enemy than for the Revolution, since the latter had other columns elsewhere invading the island. To risk all means that, having risen in the mountains, the fighters must wage *a war to the death*, a war that does not admit of truces, retreats, or compromises. To conquer is to accept as a matter of principle that life, for the revolutionary, is not the supreme good.

THE GUERRILLA BASE

PERHAPS the same dangers of imitation exist in regard to the guerrilla base. It is not for us to discuss this concept in detail, depending primarily as it does on the concrete conditions of each country and on military decisions for which the guerrilla leadership alone is responsible. Since extensive military experience alone can answer questions concerning the guerrilla base or its substitute, the security zone, we shall content ourselves with stating the problem.

If we refer to recent episodes, such as that of Peru, it is not impossible that the Chinese system of supportive bases, as systematized by Mao Tse-tung in 1938, in *Problems of Strategy in Guerrilla War Against Japan,* has reached Latin Americans and superimposed its image on their conception of the Cuban guerrilla struggle. Recently, publications that circulate in academic circles, such as *Monthly Review*, have devoted themselves to the presentation of Luis de la Puente's and the M I R's* Peruvian experience as the very

* M I R – Movimiento de Izquierda Revolucionaria. – Tr.

model of an alleged 'Cuban strategy' of armed struggle, enabling that magazine to predict its definitive failure. In a recent issue of this 'progressive' North American publication – we do not know whether such persevering naïveté, bordering on the fine art of misinformation, is more sinister or ridiculous – one reads, from the pen of Huberman and Sweezy, that Fidel Castro's strategy 'called for the establishment of a guerrilla-controlled "security zone" in the mountains which would become the focus of revolutionary attraction and development, leading eventually, as in Cuba, to a full-scale war against the Peruvian armed forces.' And, they add, 'De la Puente's main addition was that because of Peru's much greater size there should be not one or two but half a dozen or more guerrilla zones.'* It follows that this alleged 'Cuban strategy' would make the establishment of a security zone the point of departure and the first objective of the guerrilla group.

That an intellectual, especially if he is a bourgeois, should speak of strategy before all else, is normal. Unfortunately, however, the right road, the only feasible one, sets out from tactical data, rising gradually towards the definition of strategy. The abuse of strategy and the lack of tactics is a delightful vice, characteristic of the contemplative man – a vice to which we, by writing these lines, must also plead guilty. All the more reason to remain aware of the *inversion* of which we are victims when we read theoretical works. They present to us in the form of principles and a rigid framework certain so-called strategic concepts which in reality are the result of a series of experiments of a tactical nature. Thus it is that we take a result for a point of departure. For a revolutionary group, military strategy springs first of all from a combination of political and social circumstances, from its own relationship with the population, from the limitations of the terrain, from the opposing forces and their weaponry, etc. Only when these details have been mastered

* *Monthly Review*, September 1966, p. 14.

can serious plans be made. Finally – and this is even truer for guerrilla forces than for regular armies – there are no details in the action or, if you prefer, everything is a matter of detail.

This slow climb from tactics to surrounding and corresponding strategy, along with the experience gained at all intermediate stages, is to some extent the history of the Cuban Revolution. It is a good methodological rule for practical apprenticeship. The meticulous and almost obsessive attention Fidel paid to the smallest concrete detail of preparation for the most minor action, until the last day of the war, was amazing. His war correspondence makes this abundantly clear: the placing of fighters in an ambush operation; the number of bullets issued to each one; the path to be taken; the preparation and testing of mines; the inspection of provisions, etc. An excellent lesson in strict efficiency. Before speaking of 'Cuban strategy', simple honesty requires some sort of investigation among members of the Rebel Army concerning the real nature of the Cuban guerrilla movement. When an intellectual fails furthermore to obtain information from original sources, as is the case with our vanguardist pamphleteers, his ignorance acquires a specific social function, that of confusing – to the advantage of existing forces of repression – the very public he ought to be enlightening.

At first glance the guerrilla base or fixed base of support, to which the Chinese experience attributes a fundamental strategic value, requires a combination of favourable circumstances:

– An extensive territory, which has as its corollary a lack of communication facilities in the hinterland (a condition forcefully emphasized by Mao in the 1938 text cited above).

– A high density of rural population (Peru: 9 inhabitants per square kilometre).

– The existence of common borders with a friendly country. (In a narrow country like Vietnam the most important base of support was that of Viet-Bao which was a decisive element from 1950 on and which bordered on China.)

– The absence of airborne enemy troops. These constitute the counter-insurgent shock forces in almost all Latin American countries and they practise the most modern methods of repression, including encirclement by infantry combined with simultaneous landings of airborne troops in the centre of the besieged zone, and small mobile pursuit units in radio contact with the rearguard, making it possible to locate and promptly communicate the position of the guerrilla fighters, etc.

– The numerical insufficiency of the enemy forces. This is a condition obviously met in China at the time of the anti-Japanese war, but it is simply not the case in Latin America today. Let us not forget that the Chinese Red Army was constituted a regular army as early as 1927, after an entire division of the Kuomintang Army, with its Communist officers, passed over to the Communist ranks. Even before the Japanese invasion the Chinese popular forces possessed duly constituted regular units. After the foreign invasion, the Eighth and Fourth Route Armies established anti-Japanese bases, increasing their ranks from 40,000 men in 1937 to one million in 1945. Thus it was possible for the Chinese comrades to carry out a war of position in defence of the most important permanent bases.

It is clear that virtually none of these conditions prevails in Latin America today.

In this regard, what seem to be the lessons to be learned from the Cuban experience and the current struggles?

We have only to read the newspapers to know that the crucial moment for a guerrilla group is the moment it enters into action.

As with infants in poor countries, the mortality rate is very high during the first months, decreasing with each passing month thereafter. To wage a short war, to destroy the *foco* in its embryonic stage, without giving it time to adapt itself to the terrain or link itself closely with the local population or acquire a minimum of experience, is thus the golden rule of counter-insurgency. When a Yankee military adviser dreams, we are willing to bet that he sees his airborne troops dropping from the sky into the midst of a newly established guerrilla encampment. The dream, fortunately, is unrealizable, at least in this form. In every case it is always a race against the clock between the experienced forces of repression and the guerrilla forces: the guerrilla to gain time and the army not to lose a moment, the former to learn and the latter not to allow time for learning. The *foco* must be located as soon as possible; all methods are good ones, from silent infiltration to noisy mobilization of the infantry and air force so as to disturb and alarm a suspect zone, thus forcing the panic-stricken *guerrilleros* to move to more exposed territory.

Under these conditions for the guerrilla force to attempt to occupy a fixed base or to depend on a security zone, even one of several thousand square kilometers in area, is, to all appearances, to deprive itself of its best weapon – mobility, to permit itself to be contained within a zone of operations, and to allow the enemy to use its most effective weapons. The notion of the security zone raised to a fetish is the fixed encampment set up in reputedly inaccessible spots. This reliance on the characteristics of the terrain alone is always dangerous; after all, no place is inaccessible; if anyone has been able to reach it, then so can the enemy. The rule of conduct observed by the Rebel Army from the beginning was to operate as if the enemy always knew where the guerrilla force was and as if an attack would be mounted from the nearest military post. The struggle against infiltration and betrayal in Cuba thus tended to take the form of extreme mobility. Since every individual who left an encampment was considered to be a potential source of betrayal, voluntary or forced, camp sites were unavoidably temporary and subject to constant shifting during the first stage.

At the end of 1957 two columns were operating in the Sierra Maestra: Fidel's, with 120 men, and the one entrusted by him to Che – known as Column Four to confuse the enemy – consisting of 40 men. In October Che attempted, with his column then numbering 60 men, to establish the bases of a free territory in the Hombrito Valley. He set up a permanent encampment, constructed a bread oven, a shoe repair shop, and a hospital. He had a mimeograph machine sent in, with which he published the first numbers of *El Cubano Libre;* and, according to his own words, he began making plans for a small electric plant on the river of the valley. After a few weeks Sánchez Mosquera's troops attacked the base, which could not be saved even though its defence had been planned. The rebels did not have sufficient strength for its defence. Che was wounded in the foot and had to withdraw into the interior. This attempt to create a base had no serious repercussions because Fidel's column was in the vicinity and could give support to Che's column. Had it been an isolated *foco*, the results might well have been disastrous. As it turned out, the dogged defence of Hombrito forced the army to withdraw later and converted the destruction of the base into another victory. The idea of a base was correct, but premature.

It was only in April 1958, after seventeen months of continuous fighting, that the rebels set up a firm guerrilla base in the centre of the Sierra Maestra. During all that time the zone of operations was the only guerrilla base, and it was the uninterrupted offensive, carried on beyond its borders, that succeeded in 'liberating' a small part of the Sierra Maestra. The columns moved closer and closer to the lowlands, steadily expanding their forays and preventing, little by little, the penetration of the mountain range by the repressive troops. The inhabitants of the Sierra no longer had to worry about being caught up in a pincer movement between Batista's troops and the *guerilleros*. Thus it appears that the Sierra Maestra base grew from the outside in, from the periphery towards the centre.

The small basic territory then cleared was the terrain on which were to be found the field hospital, small handicraft industries, military repair shops, a radio station, a training centre for recruits, and the command post. This small base enabled the rebels to resist the 1958 general summer offensive from entrenched positions. Hugging this narrow mountain strip, they were able to face a series of converging attacks by the enemy, which at one point reduced the rebel territory to four kilometers in depth, at certain critical places.* But even under siege the Rebel Army was prepared to abandon the base, break out of the encirclement, and, if necessary, return to its early nomadism in another zone.

In Cuba the occupation of a guerrilla base, however decisive it may have been, was not the Number One political and military objective of the rebels. Objective Number One was, apparently, the destruction of the enemy's forces and, above all, the procurement of weapons. Current Guatemalan, Colombian, and Venezuelan experiences appear to confirm the validity of the Cuban experience in this regard. There the occupation of a fixed base has not been the *sine qua non* for the launching of the first offensive operations of the guerrillas: on the contrary, such a base becomes possible only after a first nomadic stage of slow entrenchment in a particularly favourable zone of operations.

During this time the guerrilla base is, according to an expression of Fidel, the territory within which the guerrilla happens to be moving; it goes where he goes. In the initial stage the base of support is in the guerrilla fighter's knapsack.

THE PARTY AND THE GUERRILLA

IN many countries of America the guerrilla force has frequently been called the 'armed fist' of a liberation front, in order to indicate its dependence on a patriotic front or on a

---

* This account of the enemy offensive and the counter-offensive by the rebels was broadcast by Fidel on 26 July 1958.

party. This expression, copied from models elaborated elsewhere – principally in Asia – is, at bottom, contrary to the
maxim of Camilo Cienfuegos: 'The rebel army is the people
in uniform.' In the absence of concrete knowledge of a
concrete and different situation, and particularly if the
differences themselves are not understood, it is dangerous
to import organizational formulas, even if they are based on
a known theory. Clearly, it is physically dangerous, since
many military errors derive from a single political error, and
a single military error can result in the total destruction of an
incipient *foco*. Doubtless, the fact that the armed struggle in
Latin America has not been buried under the weight of its
many mis-steps, its fumblings and false starts, is a tribute to
history's tolerance. Meanwhile, the penalty for a false theory
is military defeat, and the cost of military defeat is the butch-
ery of tens and hundreds of comrades and men of the
people. As Fidel once said, certain policies belong to the
field of criminology.

To subordinate the guerrilla group strategically and tacti-
cally to a party that has not radically changed its normal
peace-time organization, or to treat it as one more ramifica-
tion of party activity brings in its wake a series of fatal military
errors. Let us review them rapidly: they are familiar to
everyone today.

1. The descent to the city

The 'fist', however well armed it may be, must consult the
head before making a move. The head – the leadership – is in
the capital. After all, isn't that where the political life of the
country is concentrated – the leaders of other parties, the
press, Congress, the ministries, the post offices – in sum, the
organs of the central power? After all, isn't that the centre of
concentration of the industrial proletariat, the factories, the
trade unions, the university, in a word, the vital forces of the
population? The norms of democratic centralism require the

commander of the guerrilla front – generally a member of the Central Committee – to participate in discussions held by the leadership; if he is not a member of the directing body, all the more reason for him to go, for he must be informed of political positions. It will be said that the leadership can send an emissary to the mountains, and this is frequently done. But to discuss political positions when they do not accord with the reality of the war, to state the concrete problems – material and political – that confront his men, to request aid, or simply to remind a forgetful leadership of the very existence of his men (a leadership, moreover, that knows nothing of the war and its problems and is immersed in the 'political life' of good times), the guerilla commander must sooner or later descend to the city; especially when political dissensions are appearing, and some organizations are breaking up and others being formed without his being consulted, the guerrilla commander must 'go down' to where 'politics' are made and guided. In so far as 'the head' is empty, or incompetent, or deaf, time is needed in order to make it understand the facts of that world more remote than the moon which is guerrilla life; thus, it is necessary to prolong the stay 'below' or else to go down again – a deadly risk. Sooner or later the guerrilla leader will fall, assassinated on the spot, or tortured, or the victim of 'suicide'. In rare cases he may merely be imprisoned, if public opinion can intervene in time. But if he escapes once, he will be caught the next time. Luck or 'mysterious fate' may play a role: an automobile accident, for example.

Let us not forget that the class enemy carries out *selective assassination* on a large scale in Latin America – kill the leaders, leave the rest alive. There is a double advantage to this: the leaders are isolated and the fighters who do not want to die are corrupted. The ruling class knows very well whom it must kill – the political-military leaders – and whom it can leave in jail or at liberty – the politicos – and those whom it wishes to release from jail or leave alone. As for most of the military leaders, the men in the mountains, no compromise with them is possible. All that can be expected of them is warfare: they must be suppressed. What about trapping or liquidating them in the mountains? If they are experienced, this is virtually impossible. All that the police and their North American advisers can do is to wait on their home ground until the guerrilla leaders come to the city. If they are ill they will go down to the city for treatment: if they are betrayed or isolated they will attempt to straighten out the hard-pressed politicos. 'The city', Fidel says, 'is a cemetery of revolutionaries and resources.' And we are not even taking into account the disastrous effect on morale that the commander's descent to the city has on the fighters, given the conditions under which they live, and considering that the prime role of a leader is to offer an example of courage and sacrifice. Better to kidnap a doctor or sequester half a hospital than to go to town for medical treatment, one guerrilla commander concluded. A leader cannot go down to the city to attend a political meeting; he has the politicos come up to discuss and make decisions in a safe place, up above; otherwise, he sends an emissary. Which presupposes, in the first place, recognition of his role as responsible leader, the willingness to give him the resources with which to exercise his leadership – if not, he takes them himself. It implies, above all, the adoption of an open and explicit strategy: What is the fundamental form of class struggle at a given moment? What is its basic terrain? Its principal objective?

2. The lack of political power leads to logistical and military dependence of the mountain forces on the city. This dependence often leads to abandonment of the guerrilla force by the city leadership.

The subordination of the guerrilla force to urban political leadership not only creates practical problems for the *guerrilleros* but also a sense of dependence and an inferiority complex. They must wait for everything from the outside world: their political cadres, their guidelines, money, arms, even the time-table of operations. They lose sight of the moral and political principle, to count on nothing but your own strength, and they gradually become the victims of the mirage of imminent outside aid. It is necessary to wait until the promised aid arrives and on that day either it does not arrive, or it arrives in minute quantity, or it is postponed to the next day. One drags on, waiting to see if the supplies equested three months earlier will arrive tomorrow – the boots, waterproof nylon cloth, munitions, gasoline, medical supplies, flashlights. In this way the political leaders hold in leash 'their' armed struggle, if only out of indolence.

And this is normal. Capitals, especially in those big Yankee branch offices in the Caribbean, are livable purgatories compared to the urban agglomerations of Asia or even of Europe. How can an inhabitant of these cities, however much of a Marxist-Leninist he may be, understand the vital importance of a square yard of nylon cloth, a can of gun grease, a pound of salt or sugar, a pair of boots? The truth is that you have to live it to understand it. Seen from outside these are 'details', 'material limitations' of the class struggle, the 'technical side', the minor and hence secondary side of things. Such are the mental reactions of a bourgeois, and any man, even a comrade, who spends his life in a city is unwittingly bourgeois in comparison with a *guerrillero*. He *cannot* know the material effort involved in eating, sleeping, moving from one place to another – briefly, in surviving. Not to have any means of subsistence except what you yourself can produce, with your own hands, starting from nature in the raw. The city-dweller lives as a consumer. As long as he has some cash in his pocket, it suffices for his daily needs. Of course it is not really enough, but with the affluence of the Yankees and the corruption that follows in their wake, more can be earned without too much difficulty.

The jungle of the city is not so brutal. Men garotte each other in order to assert their superiority, but they no longer fight to survive. Life is for all – unequally given, but given nonetheless. It exists in the shops in the form of finished products – butchered meat; baked bread; running water; the possibility of sleeping under a roof, sheltered from the rain, without the need to stand guard; electrically lit streets; medicines at the pharmacy or hospital. It is said that we are immersed in the social, and prolonged immersion debilitates. Nothing like getting out to realize to what extent these luke-warm incubators make one infantile and bourgeois. In the first stages of life in the mountains, in the seclusion of the so-called virgin forest, life is simply a daily battle in its smallest detail; especially is it a battle within the *guerrillero* himself to overcome his old habits, to erase the marks left on his body by the incubator – his weakness. In the early months the enemy to be conquered is himself, and he does not always emerge victorious from this battle. Many abandon the field, desert, or choose to return to the city to undertake other assignments.

The terrible abandonment which many *focos* have suffered, for months or sometimes for years, is explained not so much by hidden sabotage, indifference, or betrayal by the urban apparatuses, as by an irreducible difference in conditions of living, therefore in thought and behaviour. The best of comrades from the capital or from abroad – even those assigned to important missions, dedicated to their work – fall prey to this difference, which is tantamount to 'objective betrayal'. Many of them know it. When a guerrilla group communicates with city leadership or its representatives abroad, it is dealing with 'its' bourgeoisie. Even if such a bourgeoisie is needed – as an artificial lung is needed in moments of asphyxia – this difference of interests and milieu must not be lost sight of. The two worlds do not breathe the same air. Fidel Castro had this experience and did not hesitate, even at the risk of being left alone during very difficult moments, to repudiate 'his' bourgeoisie, which was given to making unprincipled alliances. For example, when he condemned the Miami Pact in his admirable letter of 14 December 1957, in which, confronted by a bourgeois policy, a proletarian morality was already being defined and incarnated by the Rebel Army – a morality which was later to reveal itself as *also* a proletarian policy.

Logistical dependence: Certain guerrilla fronts have survived on $200 sent to them over a period of a year by the political organization on which they depended; during this period of time the same organization spent thousands of dollars on propaganda work at home and abroad, on the support of functionaries, on setting up publications, convening amnesty congresses, etc., with a view to taking advantage of the prestige generated by the very existence of these guerrilla fronts even when isolated and short of combat equipment. From this and similar experiences the following conclusion can be drawn: it is less risky and safer for a guerrilla group to make raids on neighbouring villages from its own base, by vehicle if necessary (seizing and later abandoning a truck), in order to obtain foodstuffs and field equipment (knapsacks, blankets, boots, clothing, etc.), to create its own supply depots, burying or hiding them and thus assuring its freedom of action for a few months.*

However risky these raids are, they are preferable to pas-

* In this respect also, what is happening today in many Latin American countries was foretold by the history of the Cuban Revolution. It suffices to quote this passage from a letter of Fidel Castro, on behalf of the Rebel Army, to the person in charge of supplying arms:

'Sierra Maestra, 25 April 1958. Dear Bebo: We have decided to organize our own apparatus for obtaining arms from abroad. After seventeen months, without receiving the slightest aid from the organization (we received some aid a few weeks ago as the result of measures taken independently) it is indeed difficult to trust in anything except our own effort. More than 200,000 pesos have been spent but not a single gun or bullet has reached us. A good part of what we expected from Mexico more than a year ago is in the hands of the enemy, in Pinar del Río no less. The arms we needed so much were lost, consignment after consignment, because some comrades thought that it was necessary to open other fronts rather than to consolidate the one we already had.'

sive waiting: waiting on the good will or possibility of supplies from urban organizations, the hazards of transportation, the difficulties caused by encirclement operations or other mobilizations of enemy forces. Furthermore, they reduce to a minimum the possibilities of infiltration or of locating the guerrilla group, which is always done from the city to the mountains, from outside to inside, rather than the other way around.

Military dependence: Military operations cannot be planned months in advance, for a given day, in accord with the national political calendar established by the ruling class: presidential or parliamentary elections, Congressional sessions, various assemblies, official trips. It is very clear that campaign plans must be elaborated by those who must carry them out either alone or in collaboration with a political leadership that has a profound, detailed, tactical knowledge of military questions. But a political leadership without this knowledge cannot elaborate military plans on its own, according to its own convenience, as support for a policy of manoeuvring or of bringing pressure against the bourgeois régime, and then transmit such plans to the military apparatus 'to be carried out' as a customer might give an order to a waiter to be transmitted to the cook. However ridiculous the comparison may seem, the divorce between theory and practice, between political and military vanguard, can reach and *has reached* these absurd lengths.

3. The lack of a single command

This entails the lack of a general plan of action; it is not possible to combine and coordinate the available means and gear them to a main direction of action. The lack of a single command puts the revolutionary forces in the situation of an artillery gunner who has not been told in which direction to fire, of a line of attack without a principal direction of attack:

the attackers are lost on the field, they shoot at random, and die in vain. The amount and strength of firepower mean nothing without a plan, without assigning a principal sector to be subjected to concentrated fire or cross-fire. The absence of a centralized executive leadership – a political-military leadership – leads to such waste, such useless slaughter. The Front and the Party have two arms, one the military and the other legal and peaceful. How to combine the action of the two? Even tougher: how to coordinate the two wings of the apparatus, the rural guerrillas and the underground resistance in the cities? Only a notably coherent and vigorous leadership, armed with a long-term rational strategic plan, actuated by a correct political analysis, can coordinate these two facets of direct action. At least it must save its own skin. If it remains in the city, the political leadership will inevitably be destroyed or dismantled. The leaders know this, or they suspect it. But the force of tradition, the deep-rooted adherence to forms of organization fixed and hallowed by time, prevents the dissolution of an established structure and the passage to a new form of struggle required by the war situation. This resistance is normal: Lenin and the Bolshevik Party encountered it until October 1917.

There are countries today in which numerous political leaders could, at a given moment, reach an agreement to abandon the city and go to the mountains, thus escaping the growing repression. But, each day they postpone their departure; each day there is a coup d'état 'in the air', a meeting postponed, hopes of seeing the crisis resolved in the twinkling of an eye. There is always a pretext. Until one day it is too late; the police jail them or kill them. Then the traditional leadership falls. A substitute underground leadership is quickly set up, cut off from the rank and file and from other organizations and lacking the qualifications of the former duly elected leaders, now imprisoned or annihilated. This improvised leadership attends to everyday matters and becomes completely drawn into the underground routine.

Content at least to keep something like a party alive, it procrastinates, hesitates to take basic decisions, and leaves the guerrilla force as and where it is, hoping for better days and the always promised aid and, as ever, making great sacrifices.

In every case attempts will be made to enjoy the advantages of all forms of struggle without the drawbacks of any, to refuse to select one form of struggle as fundamental and another as subordinate. Each arm will be left to wave independently of the other, each on its own responsibility, without coordinated action or a system of priorities. This abstract policy, reformist or disoriented, converts the revolutionary movement into a disjointed marionette. In a war situation a wrong turn by the top leadership can lead to other wrong turns, in the opposite direction, by the two wings of the armed sector: legalist yearnings of the political leadership are matched in the armed sector by uncontrolled terrorism in the city and banditry in the countryside.

(a) *Uncontrolled actions in the city.* In the absence of a single command, there is no clear strategy of armed struggle; in the absence of a clear strategy, no plan of action. The guerrilla groups are cut off from the cities; each one acts on its own. The urban forces or those who act for them are not clearly subordinate to the Sierra; for this it would be necessary to recognize the guerrilla force as the directive wing and motive force of the movement. The results are independent and anarchic actions in the city which can jeopardize not only the guerrillas' plans but also the very significance of the battle undertaken.

'It is fundamental to recognize', Che Guevara wrote in 1960,

that a suburban guerrilla band can never spring up of its own accord . . . the suburban guerrilla will always be under the direct orders of chiefs located in another zone. The function of this guerrilla band will not be to carry out independent actions but to coordinate its activities with overall strategic plans.*

* *Guerrilla Warfare*, Monthly Review Press, p. 37.

Of course city terrorism cannot assume any decisive role, and it entails certain dangers of a political order. But if it is subordinate to the fundamental struggle, the struggle in the countryside, it has, from the military point of view, a strategic value; it immobilizes thousands of enemy soldiers, it ties up most of the repressive mechanism in unrewarding tasks of protection: factories, bridges, electric generators, public buildings, highways, oil pipe-lines – these can keep busy as much as three quarters of the army. The government must, since it is the government, protect everywhere the interests of property owners; the *guerrilleros* don't have to protect anything anywhere. They have no dead weight. Therefore the relation of forces cannot be measured in purely arithmetical terms. In Cuba, for example, Batista could never utilize more than 10,000 out of his 50,000 men against the guerrillas at any one time. And the Rebel Army, its chief tells us, became invincible when it reached a ratio of 1 to 500.

That is why Fidel, from the first day, laid down a clear strategy, all the more farsighted because the 26 July forces were more numerous and better organized in the cities (Santiago, Havana) than in the mountains during that phase of the struggle. The main emphasis was to be placed on the consolidation of the rural guerrillas, that is, on the Rebel Army, on whom the leadership of the nation-wide movement devolved. After the landing, Fidel assigned Faustino Pérez to reorganize the movement in Havana and gave him full authority to place it under the leadership of a force which, as we know, consisted of 20 men (January 1957). All available arms were to be sent to the Sierra Maestra; not one gun was to be diverted to the urban resistance. This was a directive that might appear scandalous, given the extent of that resistance and its genuine need for arms: a directive that led to more than one conflict with the urban wing of the movement and no little resentment but which permitted, in the shortest time possible, the constitution of 'the mobile strategic force', the Rebel Army, at the first front in the Sierra Maestra. It was to be this force that liquidated the régime, once and for all. 'All arms to the Sierra!' such was one of the *leitmotifs* of Fidel's letters to Frank País, head of the movement in Santiago.

After Frank País's death Fidel continued to insist on this theme. On 11 August 1957 he writes to Aly (Celia Sánchez): 'The most fitting slogan of the day ought to be, *All guns, all bullets, and all resources* to the Sierra.' In another letter to Aly, dated 14 August, he repeats this slogan.

The controversies between the two wings of the Liberation Movement continued to sharpen, inevitably. The two wings underwent unequal development everywhere, in manpower and in quality, and this gave rise to difficulties. As we know, the mountain proletarianizes the bourgeois and peasant elements, and the city can bourgeoisify the proletarians. The tactical conflicts that are bound to arise, the differences in evaluation and line, conceal a class conflict, in which the interests of the proletariat are not, paradoxically enough, on the side which one would expect. It was possible to resolve these conflicts rapidly in Cuba, and the advance towards socialism was undertaken as quickly as it was after taking power because Fidel, from the first day, demanded, won, and defended hegemony for the rural guerrillas. One of the few actions that the city was able to propose and impose was the general strike of April 1958, which ended in catastrophe, with serious repercussions for the entire movement. The Rebel Army command – both Fidel on the First Front and Raúl on the Second – agreed to the strike and collaborated in its preparations in all good faith and to the utmost of their ability: it was for the city dwellers to decide what was to happen in the city. The Sierra could not have been better informed regarding the situation than were the city people; for this common-sense reason Fidel did not oppose the strike. Thus he became the victim of the 'subjectivism' of the civilian wing of the movement. The failure of the general strike both brought to the surface a latent crisis and made possible its resolution. On the level of organization the leadership was reconstituted and all fetters formerly placed on the Sierra were removed; the high command of the Rebel Army assumed national responsibility for the movement. As for the conceptual approach to the struggle, the 'civilian' approach was definitively rejected. For the city, the guerrilla movement was a symbol, the purpose of which was to create the conditions for a coup d'état in the capital. For the Sierra, the guerrilla movement could and had to provide a military solution to the political problem which could not be resolved by any other means. Thus Fidel wrote before the strike: 'If he [Batista] succeeds in crushing the strike, nothing would be resolved. We would continue to struggle, and within six months his situation would be worse.' (Letter to Nasin, 23 March 1958.) The ruling class possessed all the means for repressing and crushing a general strike, but these same resources were of no avail against guerrilla warfare. Thus it devolved on the Sierra to save the revolution which had been imperilled by the city. With the failure of the strike, after it was proven to all that only the Sierra could save the revolution, it was logical that the Sierra should assume the responsibility of leadership. After victory Fidel, in one of his speeches, returned to the question of fundamental conflicts of strategy and class underlying this blunder and the subsequent discussions of it. *

* Che gives the following explanation of the conflict:
'Elsewhere Fidel states clearly: "It is essential that a revolutionary know how to interpret reality." Referring to the April strike, he explains that we were unable to interpret it at that moment and therefore we suffered a catastrophe. Why was the April strike called? Why was there a series of controversies within the movement between what we called "the *Sierra*" and "the *Llano*", which manifested themselves in diametrically opposed interpretations of the elements judged to be of prime importance in making decisions concerning the armed struggle?

'The *Sierra* was ready to engage the army as often as necessary, to win battle after battle, capture arms, arriving one day at the total seizure of power, with the Rebel Army as its base. The *Llano* favoured generalized armed struggle throughout the country, culminating in a revolutionary general strike that would drive out the Batista dictatorship and establish

Contemporary American experience confirms the existence of such discrepancies and splits between the forces of the mountains and the city.

(b) *Dispersion in the very heart of the rural guerrillas.* The absence of a single command and a centralized leadership favours the premature creation of a number of *focos*. Given the unequal relation of forces existing at the beginning between the reactionary and the popular forces, this division weakens the guerrillas even more than it does the repressive army. The latter suffers less from having to disperse its forces than the guerrillas, all the more so because the army will attack the guerrilla groups not simultaneously but one by one, thus obtaining an even greater absolute superiority in each sector than it would have had if the guerrilla forces had been united in a single *foco*. Here the Peruvian example speaks for itself.

A vast territory does not appear to be a sufficient argument for retarding the prior consolidation of a minimal mobile force, with minimal fire power which assures it of a considerable capacity for attack in a given sector. Elsewhere (Venezuela) the number of guerrilla *focos* suddenly increased after 1962; this was an artificial growth that did not correspond to a real growth of the guerrilla movement nor of its offensive

---

a government of "civilians"; the new army would then become "apolitical".

'The clash between these positions was continuous and hardly facilitated the unity of command necessary at such moments. The April strike was prepared and ordered by the *Llano*; this was done with the agreement of the *Sierra* leadership, which did not consider itself able to prevent it (even though it had serious doubts concerning its outcome) and with the stated reservations of the PSP [Communist Party] which warned of the danger in time.

'The revolutionary commanders went to the *Llano* to help out, and it was thus that our unforgettable army commander, Camilo Cienfuegos, made his first incursions into the Bayamo area.

'These differences go deeper than tactical divergences. The Rebel Army is already ideologically proletarian and thinks like a dispossessed class; the city remains petty bourgeois, contains future traitors among its leaders, and is very much influenced by the milieu in which it develops.'
Che Guevara, Preface to *El Partido marxista-leninista.*

capacity. In fact, this forced growth – cause and effect of the absence of a single command – weakened the guerrillas. This is perhaps one of the reasons for the Venezuelan guerrillas' tardiness in establishing themselves as the political-military vanguard and providing themselves eventually (1966) with a single command. In any case, that spontaneous and disorderly proliferation of *focos* – manned by untrained personnel, most of whom were wiped out in the first months – demonstrates clearly that the Venezuelan guerrillas did not constitute a unified movement, acting in accordance with a mature plan of action. Among the *focos* that survived the first offensive wave (Falcón, Lara, Truillo, Oriente) none developed with sufficient speed and strength to be able to catalyse the class struggle around it. Thus until recently none of them could act as a substantial counterweight to the scattered centres of power represented by the existing political parties. The lack of a single leadership of the armed struggle, truly authoritative and influential, provokes the dispersion of fronts and this dispersion in turn delays the advent of a single leadership.

This delay can be deliberate; that is, new guerrilla fronts can be created in order to hinder the establishment of a single leadership. But in this case it is more a matter of accumulating reserves to be used after victory rather than of active guerrilla fronts. They are not intended to wage war but to maintain a reserve of political personnel and to make propaganda for their promoters. To have a guerrilla force gives prestige. It makes it possible to raise one's voice and to impose oneself on the stage of power. Simple rivalry among competing organizations or a petty bourgeois sentiment of frustration in the face of an established vanguard can thus lead to an ineffectual dispersion of the rural guerrillas. Within the conditions peculiar to it, Cuba offers the example of a harmonious development of the guerrilla force, arising from a single central nucleus which grows naturally. This nucleus grows until the day when its troops, too numerous to be fed and supplied locally, must split up. From the mother cell, the Sierra Maestra, the other germ-carrying cells detach themselves, by natural division. First the original column grows to 120–150 men. Beyond this number, the resources of a given zone would be exhausted, and the column would prove to be too large for the type of terrain where irregular warfare is carred on – a terrain on which large units cannot be deployed. This column then begets various others consecutively, which may consist initially of 45, 50, or 60 men (on the Sierra Maestra front, the first one was entrusted to Che in July 1957). These columns set up new fronts, which later, in turn, create columns of tactical units. If one of these columns is assigned to a remote area, where tactical coordination with the parent column is impossible, the new column sets up another front, which in its turn begets columns. Raúl left the Sierra Maestra and headed towards northern Oriente with 60 men and organized a new front, which ultimately had several columns. Almeida, in March of 1957, moved towards the Santiago de Cuba region, where he later formed what was known as the Third Front. In August 1958, Che went down from the Sierra towards Las Villas, with 120 men; he extended the war there to the maximum, supported by the column of Camilo Cienfuegos who had left the Sierra with 90 men, and whose purpose was to organize a Western Front in Pinar del Río. But at the beginning of December, in view of the dizzy pace of development of the war and in anticipation of its imminent dénouement, he was ordered to throw all his troops into an action supporting Che's operations at Las Villas, with the aim of cutting the territory in two and liquidating Batista's main units, concentrated in the East.

The advantage of this progression from smaller to larger, which is deceptively simple and apparently effortless, is that it proclaims the simultaneous existence of an undisputed central command and a very great tactical freedom for its officers and columns. The stronger the central command and the more lucid and firm its strategy from the start, the greater will be the freedom of action and the tactical flexibility of its various fronts and columns. The concentration of resources and men in a single *foco* permits the elaboration of a single military doctrine, in the heat of the combats in which the men receive their training. 'Military doctrine' at this level denotes an ensemble of minor tactical rules that have proved effective: to attack troops on the move rather than at their station or at a halting point in their march; to attack enemy reinforcements step by step, that is, by preparing in advance ambushes along the line of march; to conserve reserves so as to strike against the retreating enemy troops after an ambush, when the latter are already demoralized and burdened by the need to remove their dead and wounded; to prohibit the majority of the fighters from loading their guns before the shooting begins; to cut and destroy the enemy column's advance guard by a double ambush of 'containment' so as to cut it in half and annihilate it once it is cut; to utilize long-range electric mines to the maximum; to opt for the capture of arms in preference to the physical destruction of the enemy; to keep the initiative in choosing surprise actions and the escalation of provocations, that is, to habituate the enemy at a given place to a certain type of action, and then to rudely surprise him by a different action at the same place; to send prisoners home; to give good care to the enemy wounded, etc. Thus, little by little, officers are formed in a certain moral, political, and military school, officers in whom the high command, when the day comes, can confidently place the strategic leadership of a zone or front, without the need to control their actions. They are all trained together, in the same school, which inculcates in them a common spirit, tactical rules, and a step-by-step political and military plan of action.

Several times, at moments in which any diversion would have been a great help, Fidel took a systematic stand against the premature creation of other guerrilla fronts, such as the one set up, with disastrous consequences, in May 1957 near the Miranda Sugar Central.

We had to demonstrate that we were alive, because we had been given some hard knocks by the *Llano*; the arms allocated to the opening of another front beginning at the Miranda Sugar Central fell into the hands of the police, who were holding several valuable leaders as prisoners, among them Faustino Pérez. Fidel was opposed to dividing the forces but he gave in to pressure exerted by the *Llano*. Thereafter the correctness of his thesis was proved, and we devoted ourselves to strengthening the Sierra Maestra as the first step towards the expansion of the guerrilla army.*

(c) *Artificial leadership of an improvised political front.* The lack of unity in the command unleashes an infinite number of compensatory mechanisms. One of the favourites is promoting a national front, to which will officially be entrusted the leadership of the armed sector.† Considerable energy is thrown into the establishment of a phantom front, composed essentially of members of the party that have formed it. Since one party does not make a front, organizations are fabricated out of the whole cloth, at the expense of the party itself, and famous progressive 'independent personalities' are sought out whose names can be whispered, adding to their mystery. So much energy and effort withheld from the armed struggle in order to supply a showy façade for it, even before it has been consolidated or extended! The habitual reaction. Then comes the standard response: Do not make real alliances, for specific objectives, around an established force, but offer a façade at any cost and adorn it before furnishing the house. Magnificent programmes are widely publicized abroad but remain unknown at home; their authors think they have squared accounts with history because they have mapped out the future, without concerning themselves – in the present – with obtaining effective means for influencing it even in its first phase. The Programme, the Front, the alliances –

* Che Guevara, *Souvenirs de la guerre révolutionnaire.*
† The *Frente Unido de Resistencia* in Guatemala (1963) and the early FAR (*Fuerzas Armadas Rebeldes*), whose pointlessness was denounced by the Edgar Ibarra guerrilla group (see the letter already cited); *Frente de Liberación Nacional de Venezuela*, etc.

all this beautiful artificial machinery absorbs attention and thus provides excuses for not putting into operation the *instrument for achieving it* – the people's army, which alone can give historical significance and effectiveness to a political front. We must not confuse warfare and its propaganda. No artificial front can fill the vacuum created by a lack of military and political leadership. To conceal one vacuum with another does not eliminate the first, it merely adds a second.

Once again, and in spite of all previous experience, institutions are taking priority over actions. Even before going into action, fledgling revolutionary movements or small groups of men numbering a few dozen are working out tables of organization more complex and unintelligible than those of a ministry, replete with Orders, Directives, Commissions – as if a revolutionary movement were to be measured by the number of its subsidiary units. Forms of organization precede the content, while content itself remains unorganized. Why? Because such people are not yet liberated from the old obsession; they believe that revolutionary awareness and organization must and can in every case precede revolutionary action. Let us try to understand: it is at bottom the same naïve idealism that inspires those who are addicted to the electoral opium, for whom socialism will come on the day when one half plus one of the electorate vote for it. We reach the following paradox: the same hypotheses which govern the very peaceful activities of the reformists are unconsciously applied to the armed struggle. Why then be astonished if the blunders of the latter have their repercussions on certain guerrilla struggles?

First, it is necessary to proceed from the small to the large: to attempt to proceed in the opposite way is pointless. The smallest is the guerrilla *foco*, nucleus of the popular army. It is not a front which will create this nucleus, but rather the nucleus which, as it develops, will permit the creation of a national revolutionary front. One creates a front around something *extant*, not only around a programme of liberation.

It is the 'small motor' that sets the 'big motor' of the masses in motion and precipitates the formation of a front, as the victories won by the small motor increase. *Fidelista* guerrilla experience points to the following paradox: the weaker the revolutionary nucleus the more it must mistrust alliances; the stronger it is the more it can permit itself to seek such alliances, inasmuch as the People's Army is in control; and principles – the reasons for the struggle – are protected. This conception would be sectarian if it were only a matter of keeping the resolute purity and clear conscience of the armed nucleus, but not if it is a question of a dynamic nucleus, conceived of as the generative force and leader of an unremitting offensive war. For the sake of its own salvation this little group *cannot* remain quiescent and isolated. It stakes everything. *Patria o muerte*. It will either die – physically – or conquer, saving the country and itself. In one sense the Rebel Army struggled throughout the war and especially at its inception against unprincipled unity at any price, mobilizing militants of other parties as well as the people at large against the dictatorship, by means of their participation in the war against it. Once again the letter to exile organizations, denouncing the Miami Pact, is an incisive example. It ends with these words: 'In order to die with dignity it is not necessary to be accompanied.'

This strange dialectic had repercussions on the relations between the guerrilla force and the army. At the beginning, when the rebels were weak, Fidel strongly discouraged attempts to stage coups d'état and contacts with the military. Even a coup d'état in favour of the 26 July Movement would have been a disservice to the Rebel Army: since a counterforce was lacking, a 'liberation' junta would have been able to take over and interrupt the revolutionary process. Later, when the Sierra Maestra had acquired sufficient strength and had, little by little, become the vanguard, recognized as such by the entire population, Fidel lost no opportunity to make contact with the military, not in order to foment a coup but to accelerate the collapse of the régime and sharpen the contradictions within the army, notably between the non-commissioned officers and the Havana high command. Even if a coup had been carried off, it could no longer have side-tracked the people's struggle. It would have divided the enemy's forces but not the guerrilla forces, which would have continued the fight against the military with even more enthusiasm.* In October 1958 Fidel wrote to a comrade inside the organization: 'The revolutionary thing is not the coup d'état but the incorporation of the military into the armed struggle.' (Letter to Camacho, 10 October 1958.) Since such an incorporation could appear to be treason to the soldiers who remained loyal to their institution, he was content to invite them to talk, lay down their arms, or neutralize certain units, without imposing humiliating conditions. To accept talks is already to waver; and the more attacks they were subjected to, the more the enemy officers responded to the messages from the rebel command, despite the Batista propaganda which labelled the rebels as murderers of soldiers.

Psychological warfare is effective only if it is introduced into war itself. If military pressure is eased even briefly, political pressure on the adversary immediately lacks a point of support and falls into a void. Because soldiers were dying every day, because they saw their own lives threatened, Batista's officers, leaders of a professional army, accepted a dialogue. They no longer scoffed at such a forthright appeal. Infiltration and pressure are useful if one fights and strikes at the same time. In order for an army to respond to patriotic or revolutionary appeals from the popular armed forces, it

* Letter to Frank País, 21 July 1957: 'We are in no hurry whatsoever. We shall fight here for as long as necessary. Our fight will culminate in death or in victory for the *true* revolution. This word can already be spoken. Old fears are vanishing. The danger of a military régime diminishes because the organized strength of the people grows daily. If there is a coup or a junta, we shall from here demand the fulfilling of our programme. And if we continue this war, there is no junta that can last.'

must respect them. And a soldier respects only what he fears. We may speak of peace, but only while making war. This is the only way that the slogan of peace can be turned against the oppressor rather than against the insurrection. During this time Fidel put forth the slogan of peace and spoke of everyone's desire to end the civil war, but he showed at the same time that only Batista and his régime stood in the way of peace. The desire for peace energized the revolutionary war.

The next point is: No political front which is basically a deliberative body can assume leadership of a people's war; only a technically capable executive group, centralized and united on the basis of identical class interests, can do so; in brief, only a revolutionary general staff. A national front, heterogeneous by nature, is the scene of political wrangling, debates, endless deliberations, and temporary compromises; it can unite and exist only under conditions of imminent danger and in confrontation with an enemy. But even the method of confrontation will be based on the action of each component force, acting disconnectedly. After victory is won, these elements of the front will regain their liberty, along with their antagonisms. In any case a front can assume only the diplomatic conduct of a war but not its operational leadership. The president or directive body of a front lasts as long as compromises last. The 'arbiters' can help the leaders to win power; but it is the leaders who must maintain it; that is, unless the 'arbiter' reveals his leadership qualities in time, unless he descends from the blue sky of agreements that transcend classes and sets his feet on earth in the very midst of its vulgar society of classes and takes his place at the head of one of them.

Obviously, these work methods have a political origin. Otherwise where would they have come from? From a lack of morale? Militants possess morale, an admirable morale. In the countries where these methods have played havoc, it is the comrades, the militant Communists, who have carried the principal burden of the war. Let us examine the casualty lists: almost all the dead (as well as the imprisoned) were Party members. But alas! sacrifice is not a political argument and martyrdom does not constitute proof. When the list of martyrs grows long, when every act of courage is converted into martyrdom, it is because something is wrong. And it is just as much a moral duty to seek out the cause as it is to pay homage to the murdered or imprisoned comrades.

Underneath it all there are undoubtedly old political concepts, outworn, discredited, eroded by failure, but persisting tenaciously: (1) The old theory of the alliance of four classes, including the national bourgeoisie; (2) the concept of 'national democracy', that is, of the maintenance of capitalist relations of production, tidied up and freed of all imperialist interference, under the control of the masses, who will later call for the transition to socialism; (3) contempt for or underestimation of the peasantry for whom, to be sure, such an outlook holds no appeal. At bottom many of these political organizations still lack a concrete analysis of the prevailing modes of production in each Latin American country, of existing combinations of modes of production, of forms of domination by one mode over the others, an analysis which alone can indicate the existing relationships among classes. These lacks, these shortcomings, are known. Obviously the mere denunciation of them does not correct them; what we are concerned with here are their practical consequences.

The phrase 'armed struggle' is brandished, repeated endlessly on paper, in programmes, but the use of the phrase cannot conceal the fact that in many places the *determination* to carry out the armed struggle and the *positive* definition of a corresponding strategy are still lacking. What do we mean by strategy? The differentiation between the primary and the secondary, from which comes a clear priority of tasks and functions. A happy pragmatism will permit all forms of struggle to drag on together, will let them come to an understanding among themselves. At one point, however, the *negative* definition of strategy may appear, in the form of a refusal: to the idea that under certain conditions peaceful forms of mass struggle must be subordinate to armed mass struggle has sometimes been opposed the idea that such a subordination would be equivalent to making the political line of the vanguard party dependent on military strategy, on the party's armed apparatus, and would subordinate party leadership to military leadership. In reality this is not the case. Once more it has been forgotten, in spite of verbal acquiescence, that guerrilla warfare is essentially political, and that for this reason the political cannot be counterposed to the military.

'Technicism' and 'militarism' – are these terms not justly applied to those who label as technicism and militarism the wish to encompass all forms of struggle within the context of guerrilla warfare, to those who counterpose political line to military strategy, political leadership to military leadership? They live in a double world, genuinely dualist and – why not say it? – deriving from a strongly *idealist* tradition: politics on one side, the military on the other. The people's war is considered to be a technique, practised in the countryside and subordinated to the political line, which is conceived of as a super-technique, 'purely' theoretical, 'purely' political. Heaven governs the earth, the soul governs the body, the head governs the hand. The Word precedes the Act. The secular substitutes for the Word – talk, palaver, chatter – precede and regulate military activity, from the heavens above.

First, one cannot see how a political leadership, in the Latin America of today, can remain aloof from technical problems of war; it is equally inconceivable that there can be political cadres who are not simultaneously military cadres. It is the situation itself, present and future, that requires this: 'the cadres' of the mass armed struggle will be those who participate in it and who, in the field, prove their ability as its leaders. But how many political leaders prefer to concern themselves, day after day, with world trade-unionism or to involve themselves in the mechanisms of a thousand and one 'international democratic organizations' dedicated to their own survival rather than devote themselves to a serious and concrete study of military questions related to the war of their people? Furthermore, military technique assumes a special importance in Latin America. Unlike China, and Asia in general, the initially great disproportion between the strength of the revolutionary forces and that of the entire repressive mechanism, and the demographic consequences of poverty in the rural areas do not permit the immediate replacement of arms and technique by sheer mass and number of combatants. On the contrary, to compensate for this initial disproportion and for the relative demographic poverty of many countries, technique must be wielded with expertise. Whence the more important role here than elsewhere of, for example, mines, explosives, bazookas, modern automatic weapons, etc. In an ambush, for example, when the smallest detail and every minute count, the intelligent use of modern automatic arms, their firing plan, a coordinated programme of fire can all compensate for the lack or scarcity of manpower on the revolutionary side. In a limited and defined number of seconds three men can now liquidate a troop transport truck carrying thirty soldiers, whereas with the older type of guns an equal number of *guerrilleros* would have been required. For the same reason the number one objective of a guerrilla group is to capture the arms of the enemy, not to attempt to annihilate him, unless necessary in order to take possession of its weapons. In brief, no detail is too small for a political-military chief: everything rests on details – on a single detail – and he himself must supervise them all.

Second, it has been proved that for the training of revolutionary cadres the people's war is more decisive than political activity without guerrilla experience. Leaders of vision in Latin America today are young, lacking in long political experience prior to joining up with the guerrillas. It is ridiculous to continue to oppose 'political cadres' to 'military cadres', 'political leadership' to 'military leadership'. Pure 'politicians' – who want to remain pure – cannot lead the armed struggle of the people; pure 'military men' can do so, and by the experience acquired in leading a guerrilla group, they become 'politicians' as well. The experiences of Cuba and, more recently, of Venezuela, Guatemala, and other countries demonstrate that people – even petty bourgeois or peasants – are more quickly and more completely moulded by the experience of guerrilla warfare than by an equal amount of time spent in a training school for cadres – a consequence, as far as men are concerned, of the essentially and totally political character of guerrilla warfare. There is a double advantage over 'traditional' political training, whether within the party, in trade union struggle, or in a national or international school for cadres: in such a political *cursus honorum* it is certain that no one will receive military training (except for details), and it is not certain that the political training received will be the best. For example: Cuba. The Rebel Army and the underground movement have furnished the Revolution with its leading cadres and with the nucleus of its activists. Even today the rebels are in the front lines of this vanguard, defending the most radical, the most communist, line within the Revolution itself. Is this not a strange destiny for 'military men' as conceived of by 'the politicians'?

However, in some countries, the 'politicians' seem to forget this experience and that of their own country. They maintain the distinction – absurd in the light of Latin American conditions – between 'politicians' on the one hand and 'military men' on the other. Many of today's activities reflect this dichotomy. For example:

– A certain party leadership removes a substantial number of cadres and combatants from the guerrilla force and sends them abroad to a school for political cadres.

– Another leadership restrains or 'controls' the political development of its military cadres, by flanking them with 'political commissars', straight from the city. Thus even if a duplicate apparatus of leadership is not established, two kinds of 'cadres' are implanted in the very bosom of the guerrilla group. This is bound to hamper the natural emergence of popular leaders, of well rounded political-military leaders. This attitude is in contrast with Fidel's, during the war in Cuba: 'To those who show military ability, also give political responsibility.' It was worth the risk: Raúl Castro, Che Guevara, Camilo Cienfuegos, and scores of officers, who are today in the political leadership of a proletarian and peasant revolution.

But there is a fact that we must not hide: The parties or organizations whose political leaderships have operated in this fashion – controlling their embryonic army from the outside, maintaining a duality of organization, removing their activists from the guerrilla force and sending them elsewhere for political training – are basing themselves on hallowed principles of organization, apparently essential to Marxist theory, that is, on a distinction between the military and the political. They base themselves, furthermore, on an entire international range of experience – in the context of protracted people's wars, those of China and Vietnam. It may be that they apply these principles badly; the principles are not to be blamed for that. Are we not then confusing a political principle with a particular form of organization or a passing state of affairs within certain parties? Are we not repudiating by implication a hallowed principle, that of the distinctiveness of the party and its predominance over the people's army in the phase preceding the seizure of power, on the fallacious pretext that the principle is badly applied? Or is the principle itself not valid for all latitudes? Let us examine the problem at its root.

2

THE PRINCIPAL LESSON
FOR THE PRESENT

1. *Which should be strengthened today, the Party or the guerrillas, embryo of the people's army? Which is the decisive link? Where should the principal effort be made?*

Such are the questions which divide militants today in those vanguard nations of Latin America where a guerrilla movement exists.

Tomorrow the militants of other nations will confront them.

Today they express a dilemma.

These questions have met with a standard response in the history of Marxism and in history as such. An answer so immutable that the mere asking of it in this form will seem a *heresy* to many. That answer is that the Party must be strengthened first, for it is the creator and the directive nucleus of the people's army. Only the Party of the working class can create a true army of the people – as the guarantor of a scientifically based political line – and win power in the interests of the workers.

Theoretical orthodoxy: It is not a matter of destroying an army but of seizing state power in order to transform the social structure. Bourgeois state power has its own superstructure (political, judicial, constitutional, etc.) which is not to be confused with its repressive apparatus. If it is a matter of breaking the *existing* political power and making of it the instrument of the democratic dictatorship of the exploited, it devolves upon the representatives of the exploited classes and of their vanguard, the working class, to carry on this *political* fight up to and including its armed form, revolutionary civil war. Now then, a class is represented by a political party,

not by a military instrumentality. The proletariat is represented by that party which expresses its class ideology,
Marxism-Leninism. Only the leadership of this party can
scientifically defend its class interests.

To the extent that it is a matter of intervening in the total
social structure, it is necessary to have scientific knowledge of
society in all its complexity, at all its levels (political, ideological, economic, etc.) and in its development. This is the
condition for carrying out a global struggle at all levels; and
the military struggle, only one level among others, has meaning only within the context of a comprehensive intervention
at all levels by the popular forces against bourgeois society.
Only the workers' party, on the basis of a scientific understanding of the social structure and of existing conditions, can
decide the slogans, the goals, and the alliances required at a
given moment. In brief, the party determines the political
content and the goal to be pursued, and the people's army is
merely an *instrument* or implementation. To take the popular
army for the party would be to take the instrument for the
goal, the means for the end: a confusion proper to techno-
cracy – hence the terms 'technicism' and 'militarism' given
to this deviation.

Historical orthodoxy: These principles have been applied up
to now in the victorious revolutionary struggles of our epoch,
in the form of the separation between the political vanguard
and the military instrumentality, with absolute supremacy of
the former over the latter. In October 1917 the Bolshevik
Red Guards were subject to the orders of the Military Committee of the Party, which was in turn under the control of
the Central Committee, whose directives it applied to the
letter. It will be said that the example is not conclusive, since
it refers to an urban workers' insurrection, not a people's war.
Let us, then, take as examples the socialist countries that have
carried on a long people's war starting in the countryside.
It is in China and Vietnam that this subordination is thrown
into sharpest relief. We know how, in China, the principle of

'politics directs the gun' (Mao Tse-tung) is expressed in reality through the vigilant leadership of the army by the Party. In Vietnam, Giap writes:

The first fundamental principle in the building of our army is the imperative necessity of placing the army under Party leadership, of constantly strengthening Party leadership. The Party is the founder, the organizer, and the educator of the army. Only its exclusive leadership can permit the army to hew to a class line, to maintain its political orientation, and to fulfil its revolutionary tasks.*

A practical expression of this principle can be found in the system of political commissars and Party committees within the Vietnamese Liberation Army. They are not merely political aides, they are the actual leaders of military units. On the question of authority, unit commanders are responsible to the Party Committee, which gives the directives in accordance with the principles of collective leadership and individual responsibility, to all echelons including the cells. Giap says, 'If the cell is weak, the company is weak.'

In China the Party committee operates at the regimental level and comprises some seven to nine members, among whom the regimental commander has the same rank as the political commissar. This Party committee orients the subordinate units. Battalions and companies have no Party committees, but they have political instructors, who assign militants to various company squads. The principle applies both at the top and at the bottom. The General Staff is not divided into four or five services, as are capitalist armies, but into two essential branches, logistic and political-military, the political branch having equal rank with the operational.

In the interests of brevity, let us resort to a symbol. The distinction between the political and the military is symbolized by certain names: Mao Tse-tung and Chu Teh during the revolutionary civil war and the Long March,

* *Guerre du peuple, armée du peuple*, p. 123.

Ho Chi Minh and Giap during the war against the French. Perhaps we could add Lenin and Trotsky during the wars of imperialist intervention in the Soviet Union.

In Cuba, military (operational) and political leadership have been combined in one man: Fidel Castro. Is this the result of mere chance, without significance, or is it an indication of a historically different situation? Is it an exception or does it foreshadow something fundamental? What light does it throw on the current Latin American experience? We must decipher this experience in time, and we must not rush to condemn history in the making because it does not conform to received principles. Fidel Castro said recently:

> I am accused of heresy. It is said that I am a heretic within the camp of Marxism-Leninism. Hmm! It is amusing that so-called Marxist organizations, which fight like cats and dogs in their dispute over possession of revolutionary truth, accuse us of wanting to apply the Cuban formula mechanically. They reproach us with a lack of understanding of the Party's role; they reproach us as heretics within the camp of Marxism-Leninism.

The fact is that those who want mechanically to apply formulas to the Latin American reality are precisely these same 'Marxists', since it is always in the interest of the man who commits a robbery to be the first to cry thief. But what does Fidel Castro say that causes him to be characterized as 'a heretic', 'subjective', and 'petty bourgeois'? What explosive message of his causes people in the capitals of America and of the socialist countries of Europe and Asia, all those who 'want to wage revolutionary war by telepathy', 'the unprincipled ones', to join in the chorus against the Cuban Revolution?

'Who will make the revolution in Latin America? Who? The people, the revolutionaries, with or without a party.' (Fidel.)

Fidel Castro says simply that there is no revolution without a vanguard; that this vanguard is not necessarily the Marxist-Leninist party; and that those who want to make the revolution have the right and the duty to constitute themselves a vanguard, independently of these parties.

It takes courage to state the facts out loud when these facts contradict a tradition. There is, then, no metaphysical equation in which vanguard = Marxist-Leninist party; there are merely dialectical conjunctions between a given function – that of the vanguard in history – and a given form of organization – that of the Marxist-Leninist party. These conjunctions arise out of prior history and depend on it. Parties exist here on earth and are subject to the rigours of terrestrial dialectics. If they have been born, they can die and be reborn in other forms. How does this rebirth come about? Under what form can the historic vanguard reappear?

Let us proceed systematically.

First question: How can we think or state that under the present circumstances there can be a revolution 'with or without a party'? This question must be asked, not in order to revive useless and sterile animosities (of which the chief beneficiary is the counter-revolution everywhere), but because the answer to the second question is contingent on it.

Second question: In what form can the historic vanguard appear?

What is depends on what was, what will be on what is. The question of parties, as they are today, is a question of history. To answer it we must look to the past.

A party is marked by its conditions of birth, its development, the class or alliance of classes that it represents and the social milieu in which it has developed. Let us take the same counter-examples in order to discover what historic conditions permit the application of the traditional formula for party and guerrilla relationships: China and Vietnam.

1. The Chinese and Vietnamese parties were involved from the beginning with the problem of establishing revolutionary power. This link was not theoretical but *practical* and manifested itself very early, in the form of a grievous experience. The Chinese Party was born in 1921, when Sun

T – D

Yat-sen's bourgeois revolution – in which it participated by reason of its affiliation with the Kuomintang – was in the ascendancy. From its inception it received direct aid from the Soviet mission, including military advisers led by Joffe and later by Borodin. The latter, on his arrival, organized the training of Chinese Communist officers at the Whampoa Military Academy, which soon permitted the Chinese Party, as Mao said in 1938, 'to recognize the importance of military matters'. Three years after it was organized it underwent the disastrous experience of the first revolutionary civil war (1924–7), the urban insurrection, and the Canton strike in which it took a leading role. It assimilated this experience and, under the aegis of Mao Tse-tung, transmuted it into self-critical understanding, which led to the adoption of an antithetical line, contrary even to the advice of the Third International, i.e. the withdrawal to the countryside and the rupture with the Kuomintang.

The Vietnamese Party came into being in 1930, immediately organized peasant insurrections in the hinterland which were quickly repressed, and two years later defined its line, under the aegis of Ho Chi Minh, in its first programme of action: 'The only path to liberation is that of armed mass struggle.' 'Our party', wrote Giap, 'came into being when the Vietnamese revolutionary movement was at its peak. From the beginning it led the peasants, encouraged them to rise up and establish soviet power. Thus, at an early stage, it became aware of the problems of revolutionary power and of armed struggle.' In brief, these parties transformed themselves, within a few years of their founding, into vanguard parties, each one with its own political line, elaborated independently of international social forces, and each profoundly linked to its people.

2. In the course of their subsequent development, international contradictions were to place these parties – like the Bolshevik Party some years earlier – at the head of popular resistance to foreign imperialism: in China, against the

Japanese invasion in 1937; in Vietnam also, against the Japanese in 1939, and against the French colonialists in 1945. The anti-feudal revolt was thus transformed into an anti-imperialist revolt, the latter giving impetus to the former. The class struggle took the form of a patriotic war, and the establishment of socialism corresponded to the restoration of national independence: the two are linked. These parties, spearheading the war of the people against the foreigners, consolidated themselves as the standard-bearers of the fatherland. They became an integral part of it.

3. The circumstances of this same war of liberation led certain parties originally composed of students and of the best of the workers' élite to withdraw to the countryside to carry on a guerrilla war against the occupying forces. They then merged with the agricultural workers and small farmers; the Red Army and the Liberation Forces (Vietminh) were transformed into peasant armies under the leadership of the party of the working class. They achieved *in practice* the alliance of the majority class and the vanguard class: the worker-peasant alliance. The Communist Party, in this case, was the result and the generative force of this alliance. So were its leaders, not artificially appointed by a congress or co-opted in traditional fashion, but tested, moulded, and tempered by this terrible struggle which they led to victory. Function makes the functionary, but paradoxically only historic individuals 'make history'.

Without going into detail, historic circumstances have not permitted Latin American Communist Parties, for the most part, to take root or develop in the same way. The conditions of their founding, their growth, their link with the exploited classes are obviously different. Each one may have its own history but they are alike in that they have not, since their founding, lived through the experience of winning power in the way the Chinese and Vietnamese parties have; they have not had the opportunity, existing as they do in countries possessing formal political independence, of leading a war of national liberation; and they have therefore not been able to achieve the worker–peasant alliance – an interrelated aggregation of limitations arising from shared historical conditions.

The natural result of this history is a certain structure of directive bodies and of the parties themselves, adapted to the circumstances in which they were born and grew. But, by definition, historic situations are not immutable. The Cuban Revolution and the processes it has set in motion throughout Latin America have upset the old perspectives. A revolutionary armed struggle, wherever it exists or is in preparation, requires a thoroughgoing transformation of peacetime practices. War, as we know, is an extension of politics, but with specific procedures and methods. The effective leadership of an armed revolutionary struggle requires a new style of leadership, a new method of organization, and new physical and ideological responses on the part of leaders and militants.

A new style of leadership: It has been widely demonstrated that guerrilla warfare is directed not from outside but from within, with the leadership accepting its full share of the risks involved. In a country where such a war is developing, most of the organization's leaders must leave the cities and join the guerrilla army. This is, first of all, a security measure, assuring the survival of the political leaders. One Latin American party has already taken this decision. This same party has likewise transformed its Central Committee, replacing most of the old leaders with young men directly involved in the war or in the underground struggle in the cities. The reconstitution of the party thus goes hand in hand with its rejuvenation.

In Latin America, wherever armed struggle is the order of the day, there is a close tie between biology and ideology. However absurd or shocking this relationship may seem, it is none the less a decisive one. An elderly man, accustomed to city living, moulded by other circumstances and goals, will not easily adjust himself to the mountain nor – though this is less so – to underground activity in the cities. In addition to the moral factor – conviction – physical fitness is the most basic of all skills needed for waging guerrilla war; the two factors go hand in hand. A perfect Marxist education is not, at the outset, an imperative condition. That an elderly man should be proven militant – and possess a revolutionary training – is not, alas, sufficient for coping with guerrilla existence, especially in the early stages. Physical aptitude is the prerequisite for all other aptitudes; a minor point of limited theoretical appeal, but the armed struggle appears to have a rationale of which theory knows nothing.

A new organization: The reconstitution of the Party into an effective directive organism, equal to the historic task, requires that an end be put to the plethora of commissions, secretariats, congresses, conferences, plenary sessions, meetings, and assemblies at all levels – national, provincial, regional, and local. Faced with a state of emergency and a militarily organized enemy such a mechanism is paralysing at best, catastrophic at worst. It is the cause of the vice of excessive deliberation which Fidel has spoken of and which hampers executive, centralized, and vertical methods, combined with the large measure of tactical independence of subordinate groups which is demanded in the conduct of military operations.

This reconstitution requires the temporary suspension of 'internal' party democracy and the temporary abolition of the principles of democratic centralism which guarantee it. While remaining voluntary and deliberate, more so than ever, party discipline becomes military discipline. Once the situation is analysed, democratic centralism helps to determine a line and to elect a general staff, after which it should be suspended in order to put the line into effect. The subordinate units go their separate ways and reduce their contact with the leadership to a minimum, according to traditional rules for underground work; in pursuance of the general line they utilize to the best of their ability the greatest margin for initiative granted to them.

New ideological reflexes: Certain behaviour patterns become inappropriate under conditions of an objective state of war: the basing of an entire political line on existing contradictions between enemy classes or between groups with differing interests within the same bourgeois social class; the consequent obsessive pursuit of alliances with one or another fraction of the bourgeoisie, of political bargaining, and of electoral manoeuvres, from which the ruling classes have so far reaped all the benefits; the safeguarding of unity at any price, regardless of revolutionary principles and interests, which has gradually turned the party and its survival in a given form into an end in itself, more sacred even than the Revolution; the siege fever, heritage of the past, and its accompanying mistrust, arrogance, rigidity and fitfulness.

Addressing himself fraternally to Party comrades during the struggle against Batista, Che Guevara made the following mordant comment: 'You are capable of creating cadres who can endure torture and imprisonment in silence but not of training cadres who can capture a machine-gun nest.' This remark in no way constitutes an appraisal of courage; it is a political evaluation. It is not a matter of replacing cowardice with courage, still less one ideology with another, but of one form of courage with another, one pattern of action (and of psychic identification) with another; that is to say, of accepting the ultimate consequences of one's principles, right up to the point where they demand of the militant other forms of action and other responses from his nervous system.*

We can now pose the second question.

* Let us speak clearly. The time has passed for believing that it suffices to be 'in the Party' to be a revolutionary. But the time has also come for putting an end to the acrimonious, obsessive, and sterile attitudes of those who think that in order to be a revolutionary one need only be 'anti-party'; these attitudes constitute two sides of the same coin, basically identical. The Manichaeism of the Party (no revolution outside the Party) finds its reflection in anti-party Manichaeism (no revolution with the Party): both are quietist. In Latin America today a revolutionary is not defined by his formal relationship with the Party, whether he is for or against it. The value of a revolutionary, like that of a party, depends on his activity.

How to overcome these deficiencies? Under what conditions can these parties resume their vanguard function, including guerrilla warfare? Is it by their own political work on themselves, or is some other form of education historically necessary? If we are to answer these questions regarding the future, we must look not at the past but at the present. Briefly, the question might be posed as follows:

2. *How is a vanguard party formed? Can the party, under existing Latin American conditions, create the popular army, or is it up to the popular army to create the vanguard? Which is the nucleus of which?*

For reasons beyond their control, many Latin American Communist Parties made a false start, thirty or forty years ago, thus creating a complicated situation. But parties are never anything but instruments of class struggle. Where the instrument no longer serves its purpose, should the class struggle come to a halt or should new instruments be forged?* A childish question: no one can make such a decision. The class struggle, especially in Latin America today, can be curbed, eroded, deflected, but it cannot be stopped. The people devise their own vanguards, making do with what is available, and the duty of revolutionaries is to hasten this development. But the development of what, precisely?

We are witnessing today, here and there, strange reversals. Che Guevara wrote that the guerrilla movement is not an end in itself, nor is it a glorious adventure; it is merely a means to an end: the conquest of political power. But, lo and behold, guerrilla forces were serving many other purposes: a form of pressure on bourgeois governments; a factor in political horse-trading; a trump card to be played in case of need – such were the objectives with which certain leaderships were attempting to saddle their military instrumental-

* Our description does not apply to countries where the absence of a serious struggle for power has so far permitted political organizations to escape such tensions.

ities. The revolutionary method was being utilized for reformist ends.* Then, after a period of marking time, the guerrillas turned away from and rejected these goals imposed from outside and assumed their own political leadership. To become reconciled with itself the guerrilla force set itself up as a political leadership, which was the only way to resolve the contradictions and to develop militarily. Let it be noted that no part of the guerrilla movement has attempted to organize a new party; it seeks rather to wipe out doctrinal or party divisions among its own combatants. The unifying factors are the war and its immediate political objectives. The guerrilla movement begins by creating unity within itself around the most urgent military tasks, which have already become political tasks, a unity of non-party elements and of all the parties represented among the *guerrilleros*. The most decisive political choice is membership in the guerrilla forces, in the Armed Forces of Liberation. Thus gradually this small army creates rank-and-file unity among all parties, as it grows and wins its first victories. Eventually the future People's Army will beget the party of which it is to be, theoretically, the instrument: essentially the party is the army.

Did not the Cuban Revolution experience this same paradox? It has been said with dismay that the party, the usual instrument for the seizure of power, was developed *after* the conquest of power. But no, it already existed in embryo – in the form of the Rebel Army. Fidel, its commander in chief, was already an unofficial party leader by early 1959. A foreign journalist in Cuba was astonished one day to see many Communist leaders in battle-dress; he had thought that battle-dress and pistols belonged to the folklore of the Revolution, that they were really a kind of martial affectation. Poor man! It was not an affectation, it was the history of the Revolution itself appearing before his eyes, and most certainly the future history of America. Just as the name of

* See 'Política y Guerrillas', by Fernández y Zanetti, in *El Caimán Barbudo*, No. 8, Havana.

socialism was formally applied to the revolution after a year of socialist practice, the name of the party came into use three years after the proletarian party had begun to exist in uniform. In Cuba it was not the party that was the directive nucleus of the popular army, as it had been in Vietnam according to Giap; the Rebel Army was the leading nucleus of the party, the nucleus that created it. The first party leaders were created on 26 July 1953 at Moncada. The party is the same age as the revolution; it will be fourteen on 26 July 1967. Moncada was the nucleus of the Rebel Army, which was in turn the nucleus of the party. Around this nucleus, and only because it already had its own political-military leadership, other political forces have been able to assemble and unite, forming what is today the Communist Party of Cuba, of which both the base and the head continue to be made up of comrades from the guerrilla army.

The Latin American revolution and its vanguard, the Cuban revolution, have thus made a decisive contribution to international revolutionary experience and to Marxism-Leninism.

Under certain conditions, the political and the military are not separate, but form one organic whole, consisting of the people's army, whose nucleus is the guerrilla army. The vanguard party can exist in the form of the guerrilla foco *itself. The guerrilla force is the party in embryo.*

This is the staggering novelty introduced by the Cuban Revolution.

It is indeed a contribution. One could of course consider this an exceptional situation, the product of a unique combination of circumstances, without further significance. On the contrary, recent developments in countries that are in the vanguard of the armed struggle on the continent confirm and reinforce it. It is reinforced because, whereas the ideology of the Cuban Rebel Army was not Marxist, the ideology of the new guerrilla commands is clearly so, just as the revolution which is their goal is clearly socialist and proletarian. It

is precisely because their line is so clear and their determination so unalterable that they have had to separate themselves, at a certain point, from the existing vanguard parties
and propose (as in Guatemala) or impose (as in Venezuela)
their own political, ideological, and organizational ideas as
the foundation of any possible agreement, on a take-it-or-
leave-it basis. In sum, it was necessary in both cases to dis-
continue all organic dependence on political parties and to
replace these enfeebled political vanguards. In other words,
they had to reach the point at which the Cuban Revolution
started.

Thus ends a divorce of several decades' duration between
Marxist theory and revolutionary practice. As tentative and
tenuous as the reconciliation may appear, it is the guerrilla
movement – master of its own political leadership – that em-
bodies it, this handful of men 'with no other alternative but
death or victory, at moments when death was a concept a
thousand times more real, and victory a myth that only a
revolutionary can dream of'. (Che.) These men may die, but
others will replace them. Risks must be taken. The union of
theory and practice is not an inevitability but a battle, and
no battle is won in advance. If this union is not achieved
there, it will not be achieved anywhere.

The guerrilla force, if it genuinely seeks total political
warfare, cannot in the long run tolerate any fundamental
duality of functions or powers. Che Guevara carries the idea
of unity so far that he proposes that the military and political
leaders who lead insurrectional struggles in America be
'united, if possible, in one person'. But whether it is an individual, as with Fidel, or collective, the important thing is
that the leadership be homogeneous, political and military
simultaneously. Career soldiers can, in the process of the
people's war, become political leaders (Luis Turcios, for
example, had he lived); militant political leaders can become
military leaders, learning the art of war by making it
(Douglas Bravo, for example).

In any case, it is necessary that they be able to make it. *A guerrilla force cannot develop on the military level if it does not become a political vanguard.* As long as it does not work out its own line, as long as it remains a pressure group or a device for creating a political diversion, it is fruitlessly marking time, however successful its partial actions may be. How can it take the initiative? On what will it build its morale? Do we perhaps believe that it will go 'too far' if it is allowed to become the catalyst for popular aspirations and energies, which will *ipso facto* transform it into a directive force? Precisely because it is a mass struggle – the most radical of all – the guerrilla movement, if it is to triumph *militarily*, must *politically* assemble around it the majority of the exploited classes. Victory is impossible without their active and organized participation, since it is the general strike or generalized urban insurrection that will give the coup de grâce to the régime and will defeat its final manoeuvres – a last-minute coup d'état, a new junta, elections – by extending the struggle throughout the country. But in order to reach that point, must there not be a long and patient effort by the mountain forces to coordinate all forms of struggle, eventually to coordinate action by the militia with that of the regular forces, to coordinate rearguard sabotage by the suburban guerrillas with operations carried out by the principal guerrilla group? And, beyond the armed struggle, must there not be an effort to play an ever larger role in the country's civilian life? Whence the importance of a radio transmitter at the disposition of the guerrilla forces. The radio permits headquarters to establish daily contact with the population residing outside the zone of operations. Thus the latter can receive political instructions and orientation which, as military successes increase, find an ever-increasing echo. In Cuba *Radio Rebelde*, which began transmitting in 1958, was frequently utilized by Fidel, and confirmed the role of the Rebel Army's General Staff as the directive force of the revolutionary movement. Increasingly everyone – from Catholics to Communists –

looked to the Sierra, tuned in to get reliable news, to know 'what to do' and 'where the action is'. Clandestinity became public. As revolutionary methods and goals became more radical, so did the people. After Batista's flight, Fidel broadcast his denunciation of the manoeuvres for a coup d'état in the capital, thus depriving the ruling class in a matter of minutes of its last card, and sealing the ultimate victory. Even before victory the radio broke through government censorship on military operations, a censorship such as prevails today in all embattled countries. It is by means of radio that the guerrillas force the doors of truth and open them wide to the entire populace, especially if they follow the ethical precepts that guided *Radio Rebelde* – never broadcast inaccurate news, never conceal a defeat, never exaggerate a victory. In short, radio produces a qualitative change in the guerrilla movement. This explains the muffled or open resistance which certain party leaders offer today to the guerrilla movement's use of this propaganda medium.

Thus, in order for the small motor really to set the big motor of the masses into motion, without which its activity will remain limited, it must first be recognized by the masses as their only interpreter and guide, under penalty of dividing and weakening the people's strength. In order to bring about this recognition, the guerrillas must assume all the functions of political and military authority. Any guerrilla movement in Latin America that wishes to pursue the people's war to the end, transforming itself if necessary into a regular army and beginning a war of movement and positions, must become the unchallenged political vanguard, with the essential elements of its leadership being incorporated in the military command.

How can this 'heresy' be justified? What gives the guerrilla movement the right to claim this political responsibility as its own and for itself alone?

The answer is: that class alliance which it alone can achieve, the alliance that will take and administer power, the alliance whose interests are those of socialism – the alliance between workers and peasants. The guerrilla army is a confirmation in action of this alliance; it is the personification of it. When the guerrilla army assumes the prerogatives of political leadership, it is responding to its class content and anticipating tomorrow's dangers. It alone can guarantee that the people's power will not be perverted after victory. If it does not assume the functions of political leadership during the course of emancipation itself, it will not be able to assume them when the war is over. And the bourgeoisie, with all necessary imperialist support, will surely take advantage of the situation. We have only to observe the difficulties in which Algeria finds itself today, because of yesterday's division between the internal fighters and their government outside the country. There is no better example of the risks implicit in the separation of military and political functions when there is no Marxist vanguard party. Thus it is the revolutionary civil war that strengthens the historic agencies of the new society. Lenin, in his last notes, wrote that 'the civil war has *welded* together the working class and the peasantry, and this is the *guarantee of an invincible strength*'.*

In the mountains, then, workers, peasants, and intellectuals meet for the first time. Their integration is not so easy at the beginning. Just as there are divisions into classes elsewhere, groups can arise even in the midst of an encampment. The peasants, especially if they are of Indian origin, stay to themselves and speak their own language (Quechua or Cakchiquel) among themselves. The others, those who know how to write and speak well, spontaneously create their own circle. Mistrust, timidity, custom, have to be gradually vanquished by means of untiring political work, in which the leaders set the example. These men all have something to learn from each other, beginning with their differences. Since they must all adapt themselves to the same conditions of life, and since they are all participating in the

* Draft of a speech (not delivered) for the Tenth Congress of Russian Soviets, December 1922. Lenin's emphasis.

same undertaking, they adapt to each other. Slowly the shared existence, the combats, the hardships endured together, weld an alliance having the simple force of friendship. Furthermore, the first law of guerrilla life is that no one survives it alone. The group's interest is the interest of each one, and *vice versa*. To live and conquer is to live and conquer all together. If a single combatant lags behind a marching column, it affects the speed and security of the entire column. In the rear is the enemy: impossible to leave the comrade behind or send him home. It is up to everyone, then, to share the burden, lighten his knapsack or cartridge-case, and help him all the way. Under these conditions class egoism does not long endure. Petty-bourgeois psychology melts like snow under the summer sun, undermining the ideology of the same stratum. Where else could such an encounter, such an alliance, take place? By the same token, the only conceivable line for a guerrilla group to adopt is the 'mass line'; it can live only with their support, in daily contact with them. Bureaucratic faintheartedness becomes irrelevant. Is this not the best education for a future socialist leader or cadre? Revolutionaries make revolutionary civil wars; but to an even greater extent it is revolutionary civil war that makes revolutionaries.

Lenin wrote: 'The civil war has educated and tempered (Denikin and the others are good *teachers*; they have taught well; *all our best militants have been in the army*).'*

The best teacher of Marxism-Leninism is the enemy, in face-to-face confrontation during the people's war. Study and apprenticeship are necessary but not decisive. There are no academy-trained cadres. One cannot claim to train revolutionary cadres in theoretical schools detached from instructional work and common combat experiences. To think otherwise would be justifiable naïveté in Western Europe; elsewhere it is unpardonable nonsense.

The guerrilla group's exercise of, or commitment to estab-

* ibid., Lenin's emphasis.

lish, a political leadership is even more clearly revealed when it organizes its first liberated zone. It then tries out and tests tomorrow's revolutionary measures (as on the Second Front in Oriente): agrarian reform, peasant congresses, levying of taxes, revolutionary tribunals, the discipline of collective life. The liberated zone becomes the prototype and the model for the future state, its administrators the models for future leaders of state. Who but a popular armed force can carry through such socialist 'rehearsals'?

The worker-peasant alliance often finds its connecting link in a group of revolutionaries of bourgeois extraction, from which a substantial part of the guerrilla command is recruited. Even if today this tendency is decreasing, because of the extreme polarization of social classes, it is far from having been eliminated.

Such is the law of 'equivalent-substitutions' in countries that have been colonized even to a limited extent: one finds that a working class of restricted size or under the influence of a reformist trade union aristocracy, and an isolated and humiliated peasantry, are willing to accept this group, of bourgeois origin, as their political leadership. In the course of the struggle which awakens and mobilizes them, a kind of provisional delegation of powers is produced.* Inversely, in order to assume this function, this historic vicarship, and in order not to usurp a role to which they have only a provisional title, this progressive petty bourgeoisie must, to use Amilcar Cabral's phrase, 'commit suicide as a class in order to be restored to life as revolutionary workers, totally identified with the deepest aspirations of their people'. The most favourable time and place for this suicide is with the guerrillas, during guerrilla action: here the small initial groups from the cities have their first daily contact with rural realities, little by little adjust themselves to its demands, and begin to understand from the inside the aspirations of their

* On this subject see 'Tercer Mundo e Ideología', by Rachid, in *El Caimán Barbudo* No. 2 (Havana).

people; they cast aside political verbosity and make of these aspirations their programme of action. Where better than in the guerrilla army could this shedding of skin and this resurrection take place?

Here the political word is abruptly made flesh. The revolutionary ideal emerges from the grey shadow of formula and acquires substance in the full light of day. This transubstantiation comes as a surprise, and when those who have experienced it want to describe it – in China, in Vietnam, in Cuba, in many places – they resort not to words but to exclamations.

The renovating spirit, the longing for collective excellence, the awareness of a higher destiny are in full flower and can develop considerably further. We had heard of these things, which had a flavour of verbal abstraction, and we accepted their beautiful meaning, but now we are living it, we are experiencing it in every sense, and it is truly unique. We have seen its incredible development in this Sierra, which is our small universe. Here the word 'people', which is so often utilized in a vague and confused sense, becomes a living, wonderful and dazzling reality. *Now* I know who the people are: I see them in that invincible force that surrounds us everywhere, I see them in the bands of thirty or forty men, lighting their way with lanterns, who descend the muddy slopes at two or three in the morning, with 30 kilos on their backs, in order to supply us with food. Who has organized them so wonderfully? Where did they acquire so much ability, astuteness, courage, self-sacrifice? No one knows! It is almost a mystery! They organize themselves all alone, spontaneously! When weary animals drop to the ground, unable to go further, men appear from all directions and carry the goods. Force cannot defeat them. It would be necessary to kill them all, to the last peasant, and that is impossible; this the dictatorship cannot do; the people are aware of it and are daily more aware of their own growing strength.*

* From Fidel Castro's last letter to Frank País, written in the Sierra Maestra, 21 July 1957. The same wonderment is expressed today in the letters of Turcios, Douglas Bravo, Camilo Torres, and others. Of course this does not mean that it is easy to obtain peasant support immediately; but when it is obtained it performs wonders. Fidel wrote the letter after eight months in the Sierra and after having escaped betrayal by several peasants.

All these factors, operating together, gave shape to a strange band which was made to appear picturesque by certain photographs and which, because of our stupidity, impressed us only through the attire and long beards of its members. These are the militants of our time, not martyrs, not functionaries, but fighters. Neither creatures of an apparatus nor potentates: at this stage, they themselves are the apparatus. Aggressive men, especially in retreat. Resolute and responsible, each of them knowing the meaning and goal of this armed class struggle through its leaders, fighters like themselves whom they see daily carrying the same packs on their backs, suffering the same blistered feet and the same thirst during a march. The blasé will smile at this vision à la Rousseau. We need not point out here that it is not love of nature nor the pursuit of happiness which brought them to the mountain, but the awareness of a historic necessity. Power is seized and held in the capital, but the road that leads the exploited to it must pass through the countryside. Need we recall that war and military discipline are characterized by rigours unknown to the *Social Contract*? This is even truer for guerrilla armies than for regular armies. Today some of these groups have disappeared before assuming a vanguard role, having retreated or suffered liquidation. In a struggle of this kind, which involves such grave risks and is still only in the process of taking its first faltering steps, such defeats are normal. Other groups, the most important ones operating in countries whose history proves their importance for all Latin America – Venezuela, Guatemala, Colombia – have established themselves and are moving ahead. It is there, in such countries as these, that history is on the march today. Tomorrow other countries will join and supersede them in the vanguard role.

Has it been noted that nearly all of these guerrilla movements neither have nor want political commissars? The majority of the fighters come from Communist ranks. These are the first socialist guerrilla forces that have not adopted the system of political commissars, a system which does not appear to correspond to the Latin American reality.

If what we have said makes any sense at all, this absence of specialists in political affairs has the effect of sanctioning the absence of specialists in military affairs. The people's army is its own political authority. The *guerrilleros* play both roles, indivisibly. Its commanders are political instructors for the fighters, its political instructors are its commanders.

Let us sum up. Not to understand perfectly the theoretical and historical novelty of this situation is to open the way to dangerous errors at the very core of the armed struggle. To consider the existing party as different from and superior to the new type of party that grows along with the guerrilla force leads logically to two attitudes.

1. *The guerrilla force should be subordinated to the party*. The system of political commissars is a consequence of this subordination. It implies that the guerrilla army is incapable of leading itself and that it must be guided from outside; that is, it presupposes the existence of a leader, someone who can bring revolutionary orientation from a previously existing vanguard. This hypothesis, unfortunately, does not correspond to reality.

2. *The guerrilla force should be an imitation of the party.* In other words, the popular army should be built on the traditional party model. We have observed one effect of this system in the preference given to organizational matters over operational tasks, in the belief that the organism can create the function. Another consequence is seen in the meetings of fighters – imitations of cell meetings. This 'democratist' method would seem to be to democracy among the *guerrilleros* what parliament is to socialist democracy (or pop art is to popular art): more than uprooting and transplanting a basically alien form, it is a dangerous graft. Naturally, meetings for political and ideological discussion among the combatants must be encouraged and fostered. But there are

decisions that belong to the command, which presumably possesses clear and sound judgement in the military and disciplinary domain. To organize meetings at every turn leads the fighters to lose confidence in the command and, ultimately, in themselves; conscious discipline is relaxed; discord and dissension are spread among the troops; a substantial part of their military effectiveness is sacrificed. We learn from accounts of the war in Spain that Republican fighters sometimes discussed official orders at the height of a battle, refusing to attack a certain position or fall back at a given moment, holding meetings on questions of tactics while under enemy fire. We know the results only too well. In Cuba this method, occasionally adopted at the beginning of the war, led to confusion and desertions from the guerrilla group on the occasion of a public trial which almost cost the life of a highly respected captain, whose gun had gone off accidentally and killed a comrade. One could cite many other similar experiences.

A new situation calls for new methods. That is to say, we must guard against adopting forms of action, whether from error or tradition, which are inappropriate to this new content.

We can now resolve the initial dilemma. In the long run, certain regions of America, for dialectical reasons, will not need to choose between a vanguard party and a popular army. But for the moment there is a historically based *order of tasks. The people's army will be the nucleus of the party, not vice versa.* The guerrilla force is the political vanguard *in nuce* and from its development a real party can arise.

That is why the guerrilla force must be developed if the political vanguard is to be developed.

That is why, at the present juncture, *the principal stress must be laid on the development of guerrilla warfare and not on the strengthening of existing parties or the creation of new parties.*

That is why *insurrectional activity is today the number one political activity.*

3

SOME CONSEQUENCES
FOR THE FUTURE

HENCE a line of action.

Hence a historic responsibility which the Cuban Revolution has never hesitated to accept.

When Comrade Che Guevara once again took up insurrectional work, he accepted on an international level the consequences of the line of action of which Fidel Castro, the leader of the Cuban Revolution, is the incarnation.

When Che Guevara reappears, it is hardly risky to assert that it will be as the head of a guerrilla movement, *as its unquestioned political and military leader*.

Today anyone can outline the general consequences of this contribution by Cuba to Latin America.

1. The setting up of military *focos*, not political '*focos*', is decisive for the future. This distinction, crucial in terms of its practical consequences, is much more than a simple difference. Between military *focos* and political '*focos*' there is not only the difference between the less and the more urgent, the less and the more decisive: *this* difference will be conceded by everyone, beginning with those who have thought they could prepare the opening of an insurrectional front by first opening a political front, 'Marxist-Leninist' or nationalist, according to the classical rules. No: it is a matter of *a new dialectic of tasks*. In order to express it schematically let us say that one must go from the military *foco* to the political movement – a natural extension of an essentially political armed struggle; but only very exceptionally does one go from a 'pure' political movement to the military *foco*. One does not vanquish the bourgeoisie on its own terrain. In most countries where conditions for armed struggle exist it is possible to move from a military *foco* to a

political *foco*, but to move in the opposite direction is virtually impossible.

Hence the oft-repeated classic involution: a new revolutionary organization appears on the scene. It aspires to legal existence and then to participation in 'normal' political life for a certain time, in order to consolidate and make a name for itself and thus prepare the conditions for armed struggle. But, lo and behold, it is gradually absorbed, swallowed up by the routine of this public political life, which becomes the stage for its normal activities. It recruits a few members, a few activists, holds its first congress, mimeographs a newspaper and various bulletins. Then come the hundred annual assemblies, the thousand rallies, the 'first international contacts', the sending abroad of delegates (for there are many congresses to be attended), permanent representation with other organizations to be arranged, public relations to be maintained. The balance sheet is always positive: functionaries function, printing presses print, delegates travel, international friendships grow, leaders are overwhelmed with work; in brief, the machine is in motion. It has cost dearly and it must be cared for. The organization is 'growing stronger'.

The prospects of insurrectional struggle diminish, delayed first for a few months then for years. Time passes, with its vicissitudes, and there is an increasing tendency to view the opening of hostilities as a somewhat sacrilegious temptation, a kind of adventurism, perennially 'premature'. True, the militants who may grow restless and ask for an explanation must be pacified; then a small annual contingent of 'military cadres' will be organized – a matter to be handled by the Top Leadership but known to the organization's activists, who whisper their hopes to each other. Alas, the moment has not yet come, there are always unforeseen factors. The militants must understand that to enter into armed struggle at a given moment would be to destroy the sacred unity of the organization, to sabotage its legality, to provoke repressions against its leaders. In short, the political organization has become an end in itself. It will not pass over to armed struggle because it must *first* wait until it establishes itself solidly as the party of the vanguard, even though in reality it cannot expect recognition of its vanguard status except through armed struggle. This vicious circle has plagued the revolutionary struggle for years.

Consequently it is useless to create antibodies in the heart of existing political organizations: the opportunist infection, far from being halted, will be aggravated, exacerbated. It has been proved that certain political or ideological struggles, certain public polemics, have only delayed the opening of the decisive mass struggle. The creation of one more political '*foco*' mobilizes only the mobilized: a number of militants and a handful of old leaders are siphoned off from one party to another, subtle internal adjustments are made within the profession, but this does not result in raising the level of the class struggle; it even tends to lower the level since the struggle is not based on genuine positions – non-existent on both sides, as far as the *national reality* is concerned – but on personal gossip, animosities, trivia. These changes do not interest the workers and peasants, who are in fact unaware of them; and they do not alarm the ruling class at all. Rather they localize the focus of infection. The capital's midtown area abounds with congresses, public lectures, bulletins, posters, all completely legal; meanwhile, in these same countries these same governments ferret out 'activists', not so noisy but deemed more dangerous.

Antibodies must be created at the base, at the level of the masses, by offering them a real alternative within their reach. Only then will the existing political leaderships be changed. In most Latin American countries it is only when the armed struggle has begun or is about to begin that the process of removing the revolution from its ghetto, from the level of academic talk-fests, from a caste of permanent globe-trotters, can get under way. In philosophical language, a certain *problématique* has vanished since the Cuban Revolution, that is to say, a certain way of posing questions which governs the meaning of all possible answers. And it is not the answers that must be changed, but the questions themselves. These 'Marxist-Leninist' fractions or parties operate within the *problématique* which is imposed by the bourgeoisie; instead of transforming it, they have contributed to its firmer entrenchment; they are bogged down in false problems and are accomplices of the opportunistic *problématique*, quarrels over precedence or office-holding in left organizations, electoral fronts, trade union manoeuvres, blackmail against their own members. This is what is called quite simply politicking. In order to escape it, there must be a change of terrain, in every sense of the word.

The new *political* organizations – all the 'Marxist-Leninist' parties or groups that have been formed since the Cuban Revolution – were established, according to their own claims, for the purpose of precipitating the armed struggle which had been sabotaged by the 'revisionists'. They have not achieved their objective. Furthermore, in order to justify their claim to sole possession of the role of vanguard of the proletariat, these organizations have ended by sabotaging the armed struggle wherever it remains to be carried out. In their condemnation of those who have put their propaganda into practice they sometimes find themselves on the same side as the leadership of the parties they have severed connexions with – verbal adversaries but partners in fact, playing the same game. If there were an arithmetic peculiar to Latin America, we would say that division equals multiplication. This *false alternative* redoubles the evils it claims to oppose. It would be too boring, too tedious, to examine the failure of the organizations or parties styling themselves, above all, 'pro-Chinese'. At the first stages of organization they are able to attract honest and resolute militants, thanks to their programmes and their promises. Very soon, however, their method of work, the noisy opportunism of their political line, the hypocritical sabotage of their own official line on the armed struggle, lead the revolutionary strata, principally the youth, to abandon them.* They then find themselves grappling with the added hostility of yet another political organization (the fraction multiplies but does not divide). Sad to say, in some countries revolutionary groups which are in the midst of serious preparations for the armed struggle feel that they are under observation and are more persecuted by these 'Marxist-Leninist' parties, from which many of them came, than they are even by the repressive agencies. In any case, they have understood that the split among the Communist Parties, a corollary of international polemics, has occurred on the wrong issues, and that the true historic division between revolutionary Marxists on the one hand and the rest on the other is of another nature and operates on another terrain.

To condemn 'fractionalism' is not, then, to endorse one political leadership or one ideological position as against another; it is to condemn a method, a form of revolutionary struggle as being sterile and ineffective, dilatory, and contradictory in its alleged goals. It is to point a warning finger at a dead-end street and to indicate a short cut.

In America, wherever an armed political vanguard exists, there is no longer a place for verbal-ideological relation to the revolution, nor for a certain type of polemic. We are on new ground; we are dealing with new issues. Wherever imperialism is actually challenged, splinter groups are reabsorbed and revolutionaries unite on methods and objectives tied to the people's war.

Let us indulge in a little sociology. Such splinter groups, 'vanguardist' or otherwise, do not exist where an active guerrilla movement is found – Venezuela, Guatemala,

* Thus in 1965 the Communist Youth of the Peruvian 'pro-Chinese' Communist Party (*Bandera Roja*) left it to form the FALN of Peru. Deprived of its backbone, the party later broke up into several narrow factions. The same process has been repeated elsewhere.

Colombia, countries whose guerrilla movements look to the Cuban Revolution as their defender and their moral and political ideal. They exist to some extent in countries where armed struggle is on the agenda of history – Peru, Bolivia, Brazil, etc. They really amount to something only in those countries that are remote from the armed struggle, where there is no clear-cut revolutionary vanguard in action. In other words, the importance of these 'Marxist-Leninist' groups is inversely proportional to the revolutionary situation of the countries where they are found. They owe their very relative success not to the fact that they are more consistently revolutionary but to the fact that the situation is not.*

That is why it is necessary to avoid the diversion of efforts and resources towards 'pure' political or 'pure' ideological fronts and to avoid the dissipation of revolutionary energies in sectarian rivalries or feuds.

That is why, in most Latin American countries, many people think that inasmuch as the revolutionary movement can only be activated by an insurrectional outlook, efforts must be concentrated on political-military organization. *Revolutionary politics, if they are not to be blocked, must be diverted from politics as such.* Political resources must be thrown into an organization which is *simultaneously* political and military, transcending all existing polemics.

* Even if we assume, by a violent exercise of the imagination, that a 'pro-Chinese' group were to assemble fifty or so scatterbrains, or renegades, in Guatemala or Venezuela, they would not last two weeks. There is no common language between a Colombian or Guatemalan *guerrillero* and a 'pro-Chinese' from Santiago or Montevideo: when they happen to meet abroad, they literally do not understand each other. More or less the same phenomenon is found in Africa. We are thus faced with a paradox: these forms of 'anti-revisionist' organizations find a more receptive soil in Europe, in a theoretical context; there they bring together more than a few honest and consistent Marxist-Leninists. 'The storm centres' and their revolutionary vanguards seem to move increasingly away from the forms of organization and agitation inspired by the Chinese comrades, whereas they gain ground among the European militants and in politically becalmed regions.

2. Without armed struggle there is no well-defined vanguard. Everywhere, wherever armed struggle does not exist, in spite of propitious conditions, the reason is that there is still no political vanguard. (This is not the case, for example, in Uruguay, where conditions for armed struggle do not exist at present, and where there is a strong and militant mass movement.)

If there is no established vanguard in these countries, it is because all the left-wing organizations have equal claims to the post of vanguard.

If it is equally possible for all to make the grade, it would not speed the formation of a really representative vanguard to maintain relations with only one among them. Under such conditions, sectarianism would be both ridiculous and baseless.

Fidel said recently: 'We don't belong to any sect; we don't belong to an international Masonic order; we don't belong to any church.'

Marxist-Leninist parties which do not fulfil their revolutionary obligations must be prevented from setting themselves up as associations for the protection of threatened interests, thereby impeding the inevitable rise of new forms of organization and revolutionary action. By the name they bear and the ideology they proclaim, they occupy *de jure* the place of the popular vanguard; if they do not occupy it *de facto*, they must not be permitted to keep the post vacant. There is no exclusive ownership of the revolution.

'Our policy is one of active relationships with all Left and popular organizations, in conformity with the Declaration of Havana,' Fidel has repeatedly said in recent months.

It is very difficult for such a front to crystallize before the armed struggle, if it is to be a genuine revolutionary front and not an alliance set up for the duration of an election or a pact among bourgeois groups to recapture their lost power. The formation of a broad anti-imperialist front is realized through the people's war.

In contrast to other countries, revolutionary Cuba makes only one demand of those asking for her support: a claim to the vanguard role can be established only by confronting imperialism with acts and not merely with words – a condition laid down by Lenin for all Marxist organizations that wished to join the Third International. 'Marxist-Leninists' should also apply the following precept of Lenin to themselves: in order to know what the social democrats are thinking, watch their hands, not their mouths.

3. No one can avoid seeing that in Latin America today the struggle against imperialism is decisive. If it is decisive, then all else is secondary.

If the armed struggle of the masses against imperialism is capable of creating by itself, in the long run, a vanguard capable of leading the peoples to socialism, it cannot define itself in terms of its relations to reformism or any other existing political organization, but fundamentally in terms of its relation to imperialism. To regulate the pace of its action by comparison with the inaction of the reformists is not only to lose time, it is to paralyse the decisive in the name of the secondary.

Furthermore, the best way of putting an end to vacillations is to pass over to the attack on imperialism and its local agents wherever conditions are ripe. In this way the problem is inverted. It will be up to the conciliators to determine their position vis-à-vis the revolutionaries, not vice versa. It is they who must define themselves in terms of the reality and with relation to a *fait accompli*. If they join in the struggle against the Empire, so much the better for everyone; if they hold back, so much the worse for them – history will see to it that they are left by the wayside. A successful ambush, a torturer cut down, a consignment of arms captured – these are the best answers to any reformist faintheartedness which may arise in one or another American country.

Since the Cuban Revolution and since the invasion of Santo Domingo, a *state of emergency* has existed in Latin

America. The Marines shoot at anything that moves, regardless of party affiliation. For reasons of both emergency and principle the armed revolutionary front is a must. Wherever the fighting has followed an ascending line, wherever the popular forces have responded to the emergency, they have moved into the magnetic field of unity. Elsewhere they are scattered and weak. Events would seem to indicate the need to focus all efforts on the practical organization of the armed struggle with a view to achieving unity on the basis of Marxist-Leninist principles.

Those who have taken up arms in Latin America today have rallied round this line of action. All groups that come closer to the armed struggle are also converging on this line. This encounter owes nothing to chance, still less to conspiracy. No one has given a signal, as the oligarchs pretend to think. This encounter is simply rational. In a given historic situation there may be a thousand ways to speak of the revolution, but there must be one necessary concordance among all those who have resolved to make it.

REVOLUTION IN THE REVOLUTION?

Régis Debray was born in 1941 and educated at the École Normale Supérieure, where he studied with the Marxist philosopher, Louis Althusser. When he first went to Cuba in 1961 he observed the great literacy campaign which resulted in Cuba's becoming the first Latin American country to wipe out illiteracy. Later he spent long periods in South America, studying the various radical parties and movements and visiting guerilla fronts where possible. On the basis of these experiences he wrote two long articles, 'Le Castrisme: la longue marche de l'Amérique Latine', published in Sartre's review, *Les Temps Modernes*, in 1963, and 'América Latina: algunos problemas de estrategia revolucionaria', in 1965; these articles established Debray's reputation.

He returned to Cuba in 1966 to take up a chair in philosophy at the University of Havana. He was given access to numerous unpublished documents, spoke with participants in the Cuban rebellion, spent much time with Fidel Castro, and in January 1967 published *Revolution in the Revolution?* in Havana. In April 1967 Debray went to Bolivia as a correspondent of the Mexican weekly *Sucesos* and the Paris publishing house of Maspero, to report on the then newly opened guerilla fronts. He was arrested by the Bolivian police while travelling under his own name and in civilian clothes. He was charged with aiding the guerilla insurrectionists active in Bolivia, thought to have been led by Castro's ex-aide and confidant, Ernesto 'Che' Guevara. Despite pleas for clemency from many world figures Debray was sentenced to thirty years' imprisonment.

Printed in the United States
by Baker & Taylor Publisher Services